YONDE KAITE

よんでかいて

JAPANESE WORKBOOK

PRIMARY LEVEL 6

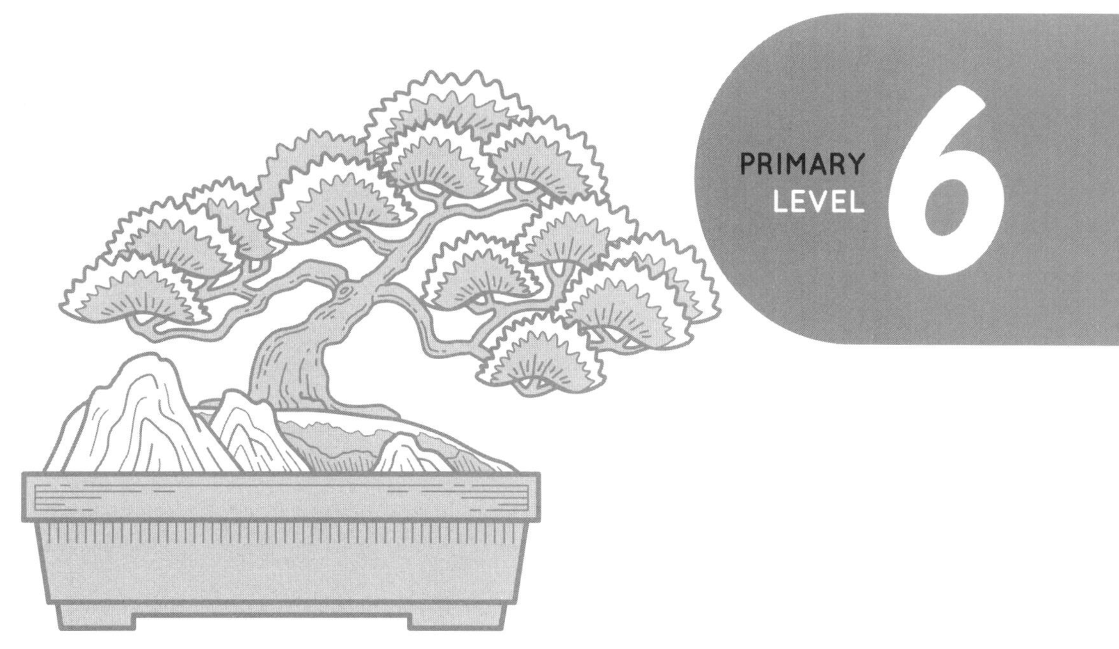

WRITTEN BY

ANNE RAJAKUMAR

WITH ORIGINAL ILLUSTRATIONS BY

JENNIFER CHENG

First published in 2002, reprinted in 2009
This redesigned edition first published in 2017

Insight Publications Pty Ltd
3/350 Charman Road
Cheltenham Victoria 3192
Australia

Tel: +61 3 8571 4950
Fax: +61 3 8571 0257
Email: books@insightpublications.com.au

www.insightpublications.com.au

ISBN: 9781875882243

Illustrations by Jennifer Cheng; other images courtesy of Shutterstock
Cover and internal design by Gisela Beer
Proofing by Sage Napthine-Morrison and Fabrice Wilmann

Printed by Markono Print Media Pte Ltd

Author acknowledgements
Special thanks to my family, Kumar, Timothy and Jessica, for their constant support and assistance and to Barbara and Chris for their untiring advice and unwavering encouragement and help.

TABLE OF CONTENTS

LANGUAGE AND EXTENSION LESSONS

WRITING LESSONS AND WORKSHEETS

日本語

何人（なんにん）	how many people?
かぞく	family
じこしょうかい	self introduction

何人（なんにん） かぞく です か。
How many people are there in your family?
☺☺☺ 人（り／にん） かぞく です。
There are ☺☺☺ people in my family.

一人	ひとり	1 person
二人	ふたり	2 people
三人	さんにん	3 people
四人	よにん	4 people
五人	ごにん	5 people

六人	ろくにん	6 people
七人	しちにん	7 people
八人	はちにん	8 people
九人	きゅうにん	9 people
十人	じゅうにん	10 people

Write a じこしょうかい in Japanese in the traditional way, from top to bottom and from right to left. Use the template and instructions on page 88 to guide you. Include your name, your age, where you live, what nationality you are, what your hobbies are, what sports you play and how many people are in your family.

Fill in the missing ひらがな characters, then insert the picture clue into the matching ひらがな square in the grid to find out what the famous Daibutsu（だいぶつ）in Kyoto looks like.

LANGUAGE LESSON 2 IN MY FAMILY

わたし	I/me ♀
ぼく	I/me ♂
おかあさん	mother
おとうさん	father
おねえさん	older sister
おにいさん	older brother

いもうと	younger sister
おとうと	younger brother
おばさん	aunt
おじさん	uncle
おばあさん	grandmother
おじいさん	grandfather

かぞく は、☺☺☺ と ☺☺☺ と ☺☺☺ と ぼく／わたし です。
My family includes ☺☺☺ and ☺☺☺ and ☺☺☺ and me.

Read the family self introduction for each child, then label the family photographs below.

はじめまして。
はなです。
かぞくは、おとうさんと
おかあさんとおねえさんと
わたしです。どうぞよろしく
おねがいします。

はじめまして。
かぞくは、おじさんと
おばあさんとおかあさんと
おにいさんとぼくです。ぼくは
ヨニです。どうぞよろしく。

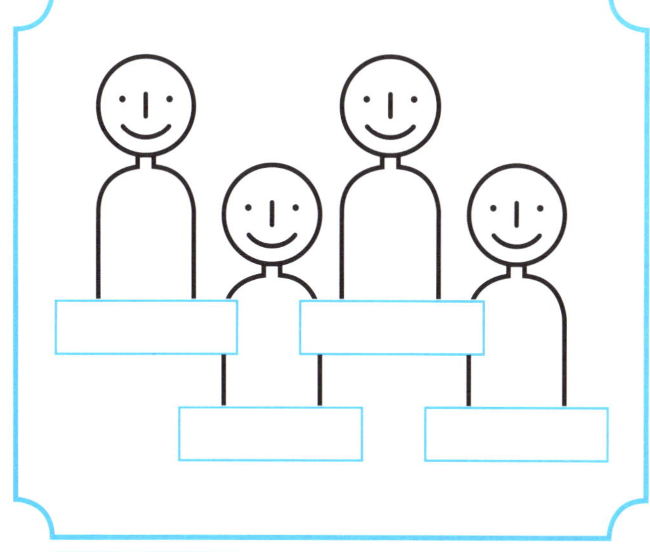

______ のかぞく

______ のかぞく

Look at the family photos below, then write a family self introduction for each of the children with speech bubbles.

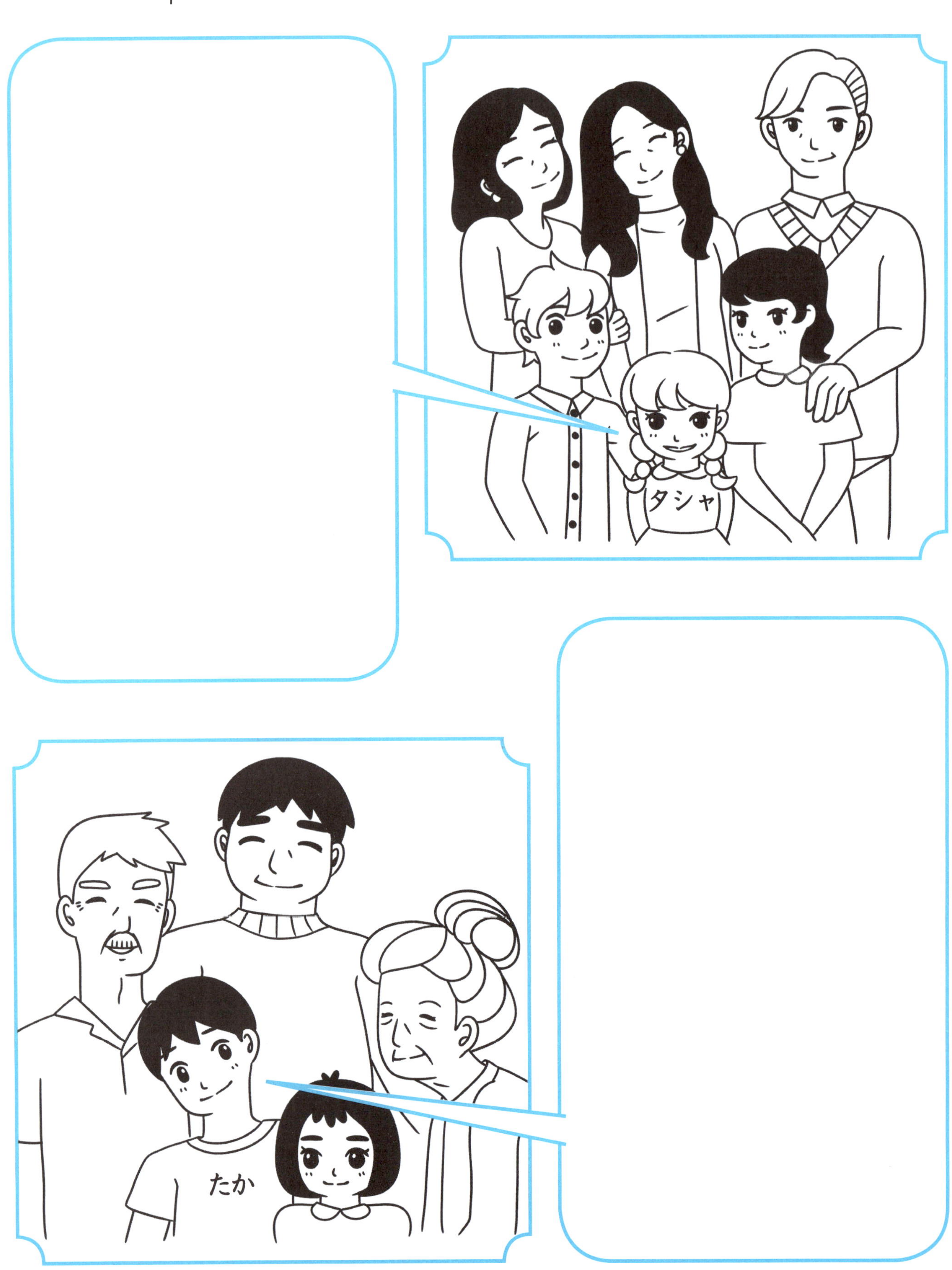

☺ name ☺ さん / くん	は
name	
ぼく	particle WA
I ♂	
わたし	
I ♀	

おじいさん	grandfather
おばあさん	grandmother
おとうさん	father
おかあさん	mother
おにいさん	older brother
おねえさん	older sister
おとうと	younger brother
いもうと	younger sister
と	and

が	います か
	do you have?
particle GA	います
	I have
	いません
	I don't have

はい、います	yes, I do have

いいえ、いません	no, I don't have

Unjumble the words to make a Japanese sentence, then translate each into English.

Jumbled Japanese words	さん　おとうさん　。　はな　が　いません　は　、
Japanese sentence	
English translation	

Jumbled Japanese words	は　。　いもうと　が　と　ぼく　、　おにいさん　います
Japanese sentence	
English translation	

Now answer the following questions in Japanese.

一　おとうさんがいますか。 ______________________

二　おかあさんがいますか。 ______________________

三　おじいさんがいますか。 ______________________

四　いもうとがいますか。 ______________________

Pipi has made a family flower arrangement by writing the names of his family members on flowers.

Draw a family flower arrangement for your family in the same way Pipi did.

HOW MANY ARE IN YOUR FAMILY?

☺name☺ さん / くん	は
name	particle WA
ぼく	
I ♂	
わたし	
I ♀	

おじいさん	grandfather	が	一人	1 person	いますか
おばあさん	grandmother		二人	2 people	do you have?
おとうさん	father		三人	3 people	
おかあさん	mother	particle GA	四人	4 people	います
おにいさん	older brother		五人	5 people	
おねえさん	older sister		六人	6 people	I have
おとうと	younger brother	は	七人	7 people	いません
		particle WA (used with negative)	八人	8 people	
いもうと	younger sister		九人	9 people	I don't have
			十人	10 people	

はい、います	yes, I do have
いいえ、いません	no, I don't have
はい、二人（ふたり）います	yes, I have two

Interview one of your classmates to find out about their family. Write their name in the first box, then record the number (in Japanese) of each kind of family member they have next to the appropriate family member word.

Classmate's name						
	は	おじいさんが		おにいさんが		います。
		おばあさんが		おねえさんが		
		おとうさんが		おとうとが		
		おかあさんが		いもうとが		

Use the information above to write at least three sentences about your friend's family, then draw a picture of them in the frame.

Can you fit a family word in each of the following word boxes?
When you have found a word that fits, write its English translation next to it.

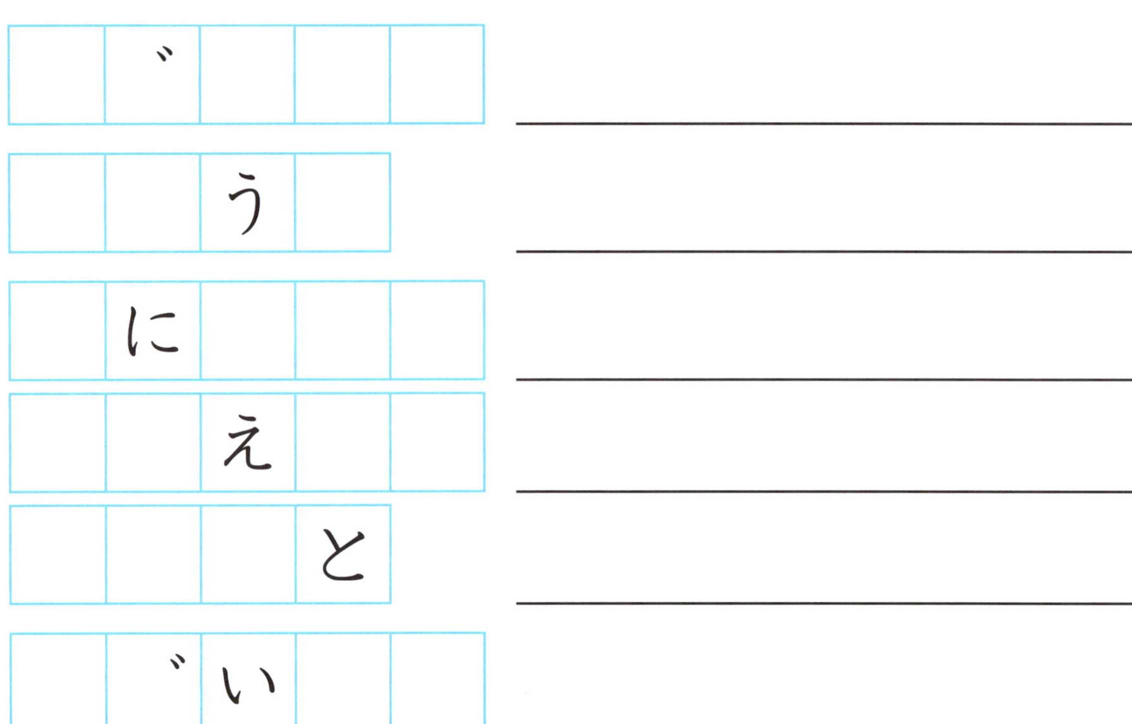

Now complete the following word boxes with any Japanese word from Language Lessons 1 – 3 that fits, then translate each word into English.

゛

゛く

と

き

ん

おかあさん	mother	は	やさしい	kind	です
おとうさん	father		いい	good	
おねえさん	older sister		かわいい	cute	
おにいさん	older brother	particle WA	うるさい	noisy	is
いもうと	younger sister		こわい	scary	
おとうと	younger brother		わるい	bad	

Look at the picture clues, then write what Jess might say about each of her family members. Use each adjective from the vocabulary box above **once**. The first one has been done for you to trace over.

Complete the crossword puzzle by translating the clues into Japanese and writing your answers using hiragana letters. Use the wordlist at the back of the book if you have forgotten any words.

1.			2.					3.	4.			5.
	6.	7.				8.	9.				10.	
11.					12.		13.					
		14.										15.
	16.				17.					18.		
19.			20.							21.		
		22.						23.				
24.						25.				26.		
		27.										28.
29.											30.	
		31.					32.					

Clues across

1. and
2. two people
3. tomorrow
6. red
8. blue
10. where
13. family
14. younger sister
16. good
17. noisy
19. summer
21. ten
22. How many people?
23. bad
24. white
26. used after girls' names
27. Friday
29. scary
30. often
31. six people
32. grandmother

Clues down

4. The smallest of the four main islands of Japan
5. cat
7. cute
9. mother
11. is
12. father
15. younger brother
16. when
18. grandfather
20. three people
23. I (used by girls)
25. snake
27. yellow
28. six
29. this
30. four

☺ name ☺ さん / くん	は
name	
ぼく	particle WA
I ♂	
わたし	
I ♀	

ペット	pet	が	います か
あひる	duck		do you have?
きんぎょ	goldfish		
へび	snake	particle GA	います
うま	horse		
うさぎ	rabbit		I have
いぬ	dog	は	いません
とり	bird	particle WA (used with negative)	
ねこ	cat		I don't have

はい	yes	いいえ	no	と	and

Read the information below, then join the child and their correct pet with a collar and leash.

はなさんは、きんぎょがいます。
たかくんは、うまがいます。
カリナさんは、うさぎがいます。
アイシャさんは、いぬがいます。
アンガスくんは、あひるがいます。
ジェシカさんは、へびがいます。
トマスくんは、とりとねこがいます。

Answer the following questions, then put your answers together to make a short composition entitled ぼく (for boys) or わたし (for girls). Write your composition in the traditional Japanese way, using the template and instructions on page 88.

おなまえは、何(なん)ですか。 ____________________

何(なん)さいですか。 ____________________

何(なん)ねんせいですか。 ____________________

どこにすんでいますか。 ____________________

何人(なにじん)ですか。 ____________________

何人(なんにん)かぞくですか。 ____________________

しゅみは、何(なん)ですか。 ____________________

ペットがすきですか 。 ____________________

ペットがいますか。 ____________________

ペットのなまえは、何(なん)ですか。 ____________________

☺ name ☺ さん / くん の
☺ name ☺ 's
ぼくの
my ♂
わたしの
my ♀

ペット	は	何（なに）	what	です か
		あひる	duck	
		きんぎょ	goldfish	
		へび	snake	is it?
		うま	horse	
pet	topic particle WA	うさぎ	rabbit	です
		いぬ	dog	
		とり	bird	is
		ねこ	cat	

わたしの ペット は、☺☺☺ です。	My (♀) pet is a ☺☺☺.

Follow the string to find whose animal is whose, then complete the speech bubbles underneath.

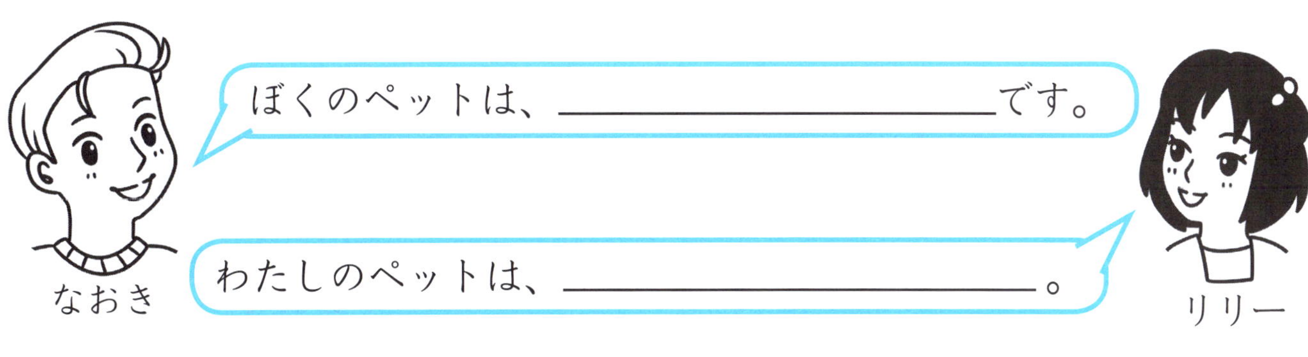

EXTENSION LESSON 7 WHAT IS YOUR PET?

Draw the picture clues into the matching squares on the grid to discover what Pipi's pet is, then answer the question underneath.

ピピちゃんのペットは、何(なん)ですか。 ________________________

☺ name ☺ さん / くん の	☺ name ☺ 's
ぼくの	my ♂
わたしの	my ♀

ペット	pet	の	なまえ	は	何(なん) です か。
あひる	duck				What is it?
きんぎょ	goldfish				
へび	snake				
うま	horse				
うさぎ	rabbit	particle NO ('s)	name	topic particle WA	☺☺☺ です。
いぬ	dog				It is ☺☺☺.
とり	bird				
ねこ	cat				

ぼくの ペット の なまえ は、☺☺☺ です。	My (♂) pet's name is ☺☺☺.

Look at the picture clues, then find the mistake in each sentence. Circle the mistake and rewrite the sentence correctly underneath.

トビ

ピピちゃんのペットのなまえのトビです。

____

ワン

はなくんのペットのなまえは、ワンです。

____

たかくんのねこのなまえは、ジージーです。

____

スベルくんのへびのなまえは、ティムです。

____

Can you break the coded sentences? Most of the code is done for you. You will have to do the rest to discover the meaning of the sentences. Good luck!

letter	い	う	え	お	か	が	き			し		せ	ぞ	た		と	な	ね			び	へ	ぼ	ま	り	わ		六	十	人
code	ア	イ	ウ	エ	オ	カ	キ	ク	ケ	コ	サ	シ	ス	セ	ソ	タ	チ	ツ	テ	ト	ナ	ニ	ヌ	ネ	ノ	ハ	ヒ	フ	ヘ	ホ

letter	ペ	ト	ッ
code	マ	ミ	ム

一　オスクト、ヘホソサ。

Japanese: ____________________

English: ____________________

二　ヌクト、エタイケヒカアネシヒ。

Japanese: ____________________

English: ____________________

三　ハセコテマムミテチネウト、ミミソサ。

Japanese: ____________________

English: ____________________

四　ヌクト、フツヒシアソサ。

Japanese: ____________________

English: ____________________

五　タノタニナカサキソサ。

Japanese: ____________________

English: ____________________

あひる	duck	は	だれの	whose	ペット	です か
きんぎょ	goldfish					
へび	snake		☺ name ☺ くんの	☺ name ☺'s ♂		is it?
うま	horse					
うさぎ	rabbit	particle WA	☺ name ☺ さんの	☺ name ☺'s ♀	pet	です
いぬ	dog					
とり	bird		ぼくの	my ♂		is
ねこ	cat		わたしの	my ♀		

☺☺☺ は、だれの ペット です か。	☺☺☺ は、だれの です か。
Whose pet is the ☺☺☺ ?	Whose is the ☺☺☺ ?

Look at the picture clues at the bottom of the page and answer the following questions. The first one has been done for you to trace over.

一 とりはだれのペットですか。

とりはマックスくんのペットです。

二 あひるは、だれのペットですか。

____

三 いぬは、だれのペットですか。

____

四 へびは、だれのペットですか。

____

Look at all the examples of topic particle は in this book. In the box below, write what you think particle は does in a Japanese sentence.

Particle は

Now see how many sentences you can make starting with ☺ something ☺ は.

一 ______________________________

____

二 ______________________________

____

三 ______________________________

____

四 ______________________________

____

五 ______________________________

____

六 ______________________________

____

七 ______________________________

____

どんな / what kind of	Pet		です か / is it?
	ペット	pet	
	あひる	duck	
	きんぎょ	goldfish	
	へび	snake	
	うま	horse	
	うさぎ	rabbit	
	いぬ	dog	
	とり	bird	
	ねこ	cat	

Adjective		です / is
おおきい	big	
ちいさい	small	
おもしろい	funny	
かわいい	cute	
うるさい	noisy	
こわい	scary	

どんな とり です か。
What kind of bird is it?

The puzzle below is called an Amidakuji（あみだくじ）and is commonly used in Japan. Find out about each pet by following the vertical line downwards under the pet of your choice. Stop when you come to a horizontal line. Follow the horizontal line until you come to the next vertical line, which you follow downwards. Keep doing this until you reach the description of the pet. Then answer the questions below.

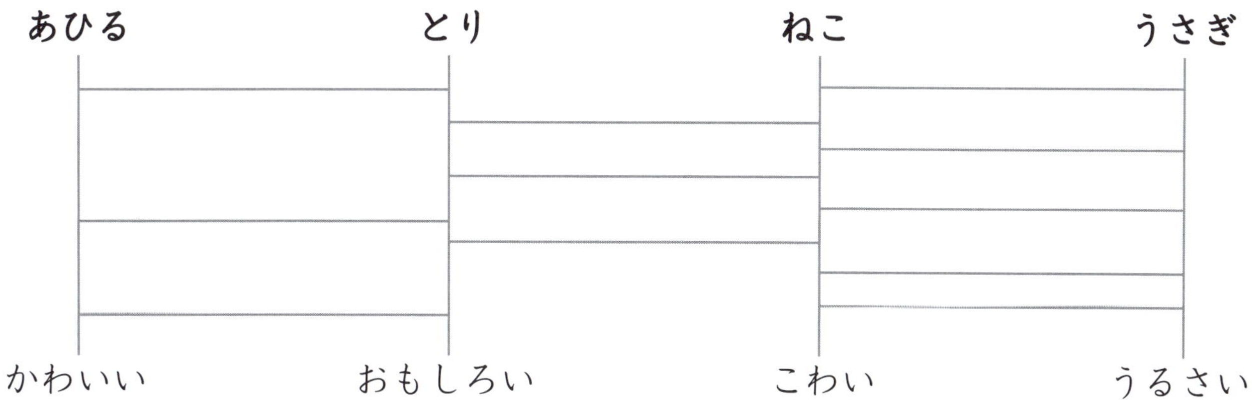

一　どんなあひるですか。 ____________________

二　どんなとりですか ____________________

三　どんなねこですか ____________________

四　どんなうさぎですか。 ____________________

Read the Japanese story below, then rewrite it in your own words (in English) in the box provided.

Japanese

はなさんは、日本人（にほんじん）です。はなさんは、しこくにすんでいます。
十二さいです。五人（にん）かぞくです。おかあさんとおじいさんとおとうとが二人います。
おとうとはわるいです。はなさんは、ペットがすきです。とりとねこと
きんぎょといぬがいます。
とりは、うるさいペットです。ねこは、ちいさいペットです。きんぎょは、
かわいいです。そしていぬは、こわいです。おとうとのペットは、へびです。
へびのなまえは、チャーリーです。おもしろいペットですね！

ね	そして
isn't it?	and also

English

おたんじょう日 (び)	は
your birthday	
たんじょう日 (び)	particle WA
my birthday	

いつ	when	です か。	is it?

一月 (いちがつ)	January	七月 (しちがつ)	July	です
二月 (にがつ)	February	八月 (はちがつ)	August	
三月 (さんがつ)	March	九月 (くがつ)	September	
四月 (しがつ)	April	十月 (じゅうがつ)	October	is
五月 (ごがつ)	May	十一月 (じゅういちがつ)	November	
六月 (ろくがつ)	June	十二月 (じゅうにがつ)	December	

Trace over the even months in the word search in あか, and the odd months in あお. Trace over the Japanese words for 'birthday' and 'when' in みどり. Look for words vertically, horizontally and diagonally.

本	し	え	ナ	ト	ふ	へ	た	ウ	す	七	し	エ	ヌ	こ	へ	め
七	月	が	コ	り	い	け	四	え	ツ	オ	っ	三	月	で	む	六
サ	さ	テ	一	る	こ	せ	イ	月	ょ	た	ち	け	ら	さ	ま	月
日	う	ラ	月	く	そ	ホ	う	な	チ	ん	よ	り	フ	み	は	か
だ	四	ケ	ほ	あ	マ	ま	ぶ	ヒ	ゆ	じ	ば	カ	ひ	九	ど	ろ
三	み	十	ぎ	べ	ア	ユ	二	月	日	ょ	た	タ	ネ	月	ヤ	六
ぼ	ヨ	シ	二	き	た	も	や	そ	に	う	人	く	あ	の	う	き
八	れ	ミ	ぞ	月	ぐ	ス	円	げ	せ	び	き	千	ざ	い	一	い
月	す	お	ち	ル	ク	か	え	ム	百	ぬ	ら	十	キ	り	五	お
っ	と	む	十	一	月	ぜ	セ	ご	五	メ	ソ	月	る	い	つ	れ
ろ	つ	か	ち	め	お	ょ	ハ	レ	ゅ	月	よ	ロ	ノ	と	あ	そ
三	て	や	四	二	も	つ	て	ず	ゆ	モ	ね	九	じ	ゃ	二	十

Circle the odd one out.

一 おかあさん　おとうさん　たんじょうび　おにいさん

二 いぬ　いもうと　うさぎ　ねこ　へび

三 おもしろい　わるい　うるさい　かわいい　あひる

四 三月　五月　三人　六月　九月

五 だれの　きんぎょ　わたしの　はなさんの　おとうさんの

List, in Japanese, all the things you can see hidden in the picture below.

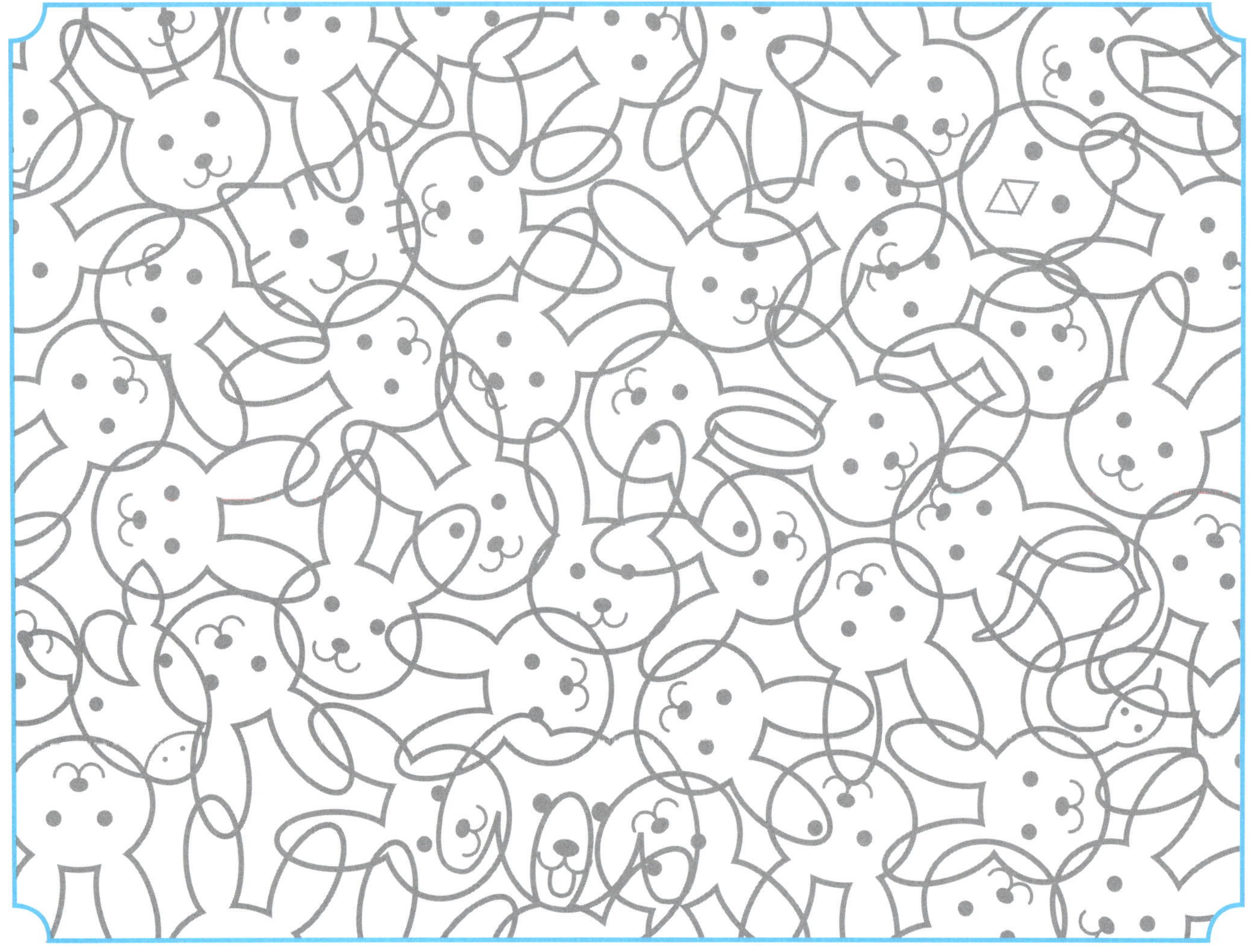

I found:

______________________　______________________

______________________　______________________

______________________　______________________

おたんじょう日（び） は いつ です か。	When is your birthday?

たんじょう日（び）	は	☺☺☺がつ	一日	ついたち	1st	九日	ここのか	9th	です
			二日	ふつか	2nd	十日	とおか	10th	
			三日	みっか	3rd	十一日	じゅういちにち	11th	
			四日	よっか	4th	十二日	じゅうににち	12th	
my birthday	particle WA	☺☺☺ month	五日	いつか	5th	十三日	じゅうさんにち	13th	is
			六日	むいか	6th	十四日	じゅうよっか	14th	
			七日	なのか	7th	十五日	じゅうごにち	15th	
			八日	ようか	8th				

Use kanji to write the following dates in Japanese:

8th June

1st September

14th May

7th January

2nd October

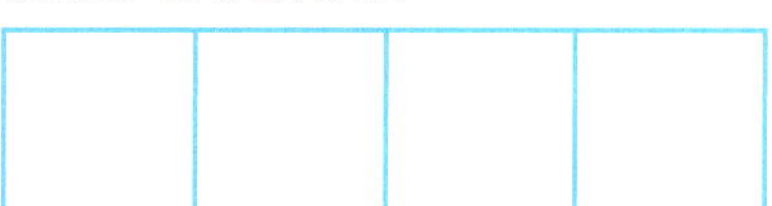

5th March

9th March

13th February

12th August

6th November

Join the hiragana dates and their matching kanji with a line.

五月五日

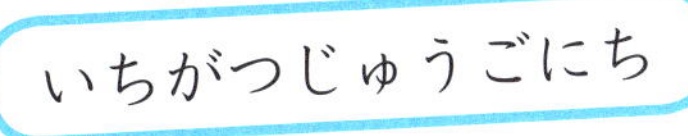

三月六日

ろくがつじゅういちにち

一月十五日

十一月二日

はちがつここのか

じゅういちがつふつか

Look at Pipi's diary for the first half of May, then answer the questions below.

日曜日(にちようび)	月曜日(げつようび)	火曜日(かようび)	水曜日(すいようび)	木曜日(もくようび)	金曜日(きんようび)	土曜日(どようび)
テニスをします。 **五月一日**	うみに行(い)きます。 **五月二日**	こうえんでやきゅうをします。 **五月三日**	デパートでショッピングをします。 **五月四日**	日本(にほん)ごをべんきょうします。 **五月五日**	おじいさんのうちに行(い)きます。 **五月六日**	ペットをかいます。 **五月七日**
グランドでサッカーをします。 **五月八日**	としょかんに行(い)きます。 **五月九日**	おかあさんとこうえんに行(い)きます。 **五月十日**	おばあさんとどうぶつえんに行(い)きます。 **五月十一日**	でんしゃでおとうさんとみせに行(い)きます。 **五月十二日**	うちでともだちとビデオゲームをします。 **五月十三日**	うみですいえいをします。 **五月十四日**

一　ピピちゃんは、五月四日(ごがつよっか)に何(なに)をしますか。

____

二　ピピちゃんは、五月七日(ごがつなのか)にビデオゲームをかいますか。

____

三　ピピちゃんは、五月十日(ごがつとおか)にだれとこうえんに行(い)きますか。

____

四　ピピちゃんは、五月十三日(ごがつじゅうさんにち)にどこでビデオグームをしますか。

____

五　ピピちゃんは、いつテニスをしますか。

____

六　五月十日(ごがつとおか)は、何曜日(なんようび)ですか。

____

だれと – who with?
ともだちと – with a friend

おたんじょう日(び) は いつ です か。	When is your birthday?

たんじょう日(び)	は	☺☺☺がつ	十六日	じゅうろくにち	16th	二十四日	にじゅうよっか	24th	です
			十七日	じゅうしちにち	17th	二十五日	にじゅうごにち	25th	
			十八日	じゅうはちにち	18th	二十六日	にじゅうろくにち	26th	
			十九日	じゅうくにち	19th	二十七日	にじゅうしちにち	27th	
my birthday	particle WA	☺☺☺ month	二十日	はつか	20th	二十八日	にじゅうはちにち	28th	is
			二十一日	にじゅういちにち	21st	二十九日	にじゅうくにち	29th	
			二十二日	にじゅうににち	22nd	三十日	さんじゅうにち	30th	
			二十三日	にじゅうさんにち	23rd	三十一日	さんじゅういちにち	31st	

Insert the matching kanji under the hiragana dates to complete the 'Days of the Month Rap'.

ついたち

ふつか

みっか

よっか

Learning Japanese is much more fun than playing soccer.

いつか

むいか

なのか

ようか

You'll need to know the days and months to be a good talker.

ここのか

とおか

, after that there's no か,

にち

is the one to use, except for

にじゅうよっか

.

And 20 which is

はつか

and 14 is

じゅうよっか

.

Complete the following table of days of the month. Try not to look up your answers.

Kanji	Hiragana	English
一日		1st
		3rd
		4th
	いつか	
六日		6th
		7th
		8th
	じゅういちにち	11th
十三日		13th
		14th
	じゅうごにち	
		16th

Kanji	Hiragana	English
十七日		
		18th
二十日		
		22nd
	にじゅう さんにち	
		25th
二十七日		
		30th
		31st

Answer the following questions for yourself.

一　おたんじょう日(び)は、いつですか。

____

二　おかあさんのおたんじょう日(び)は、いつですか。

____

LANGUAGE LESSON 14 — BIRTH YEAR SIGNS

おたんじょう日(び)は、いつ です か。	When is your birthday?
何年(なにどし) です か。	What birth year sign are you?

ねずみ	mouse/rat	たつ	dragon	さる	monkey	年(どし)	です
うし	cow	へび	snake	とり	bird (rooster)		
とら	tiger	うま	horse	いぬ	dog	year	(I) am
うさぎ	rabbit	ひつじ	sheep	いのしし	wild pig / boar		

Complete the chart below by asking four classmates their birthday and birth year sign. Use the information around the table to work out your birth year sign.

ともだち – friend

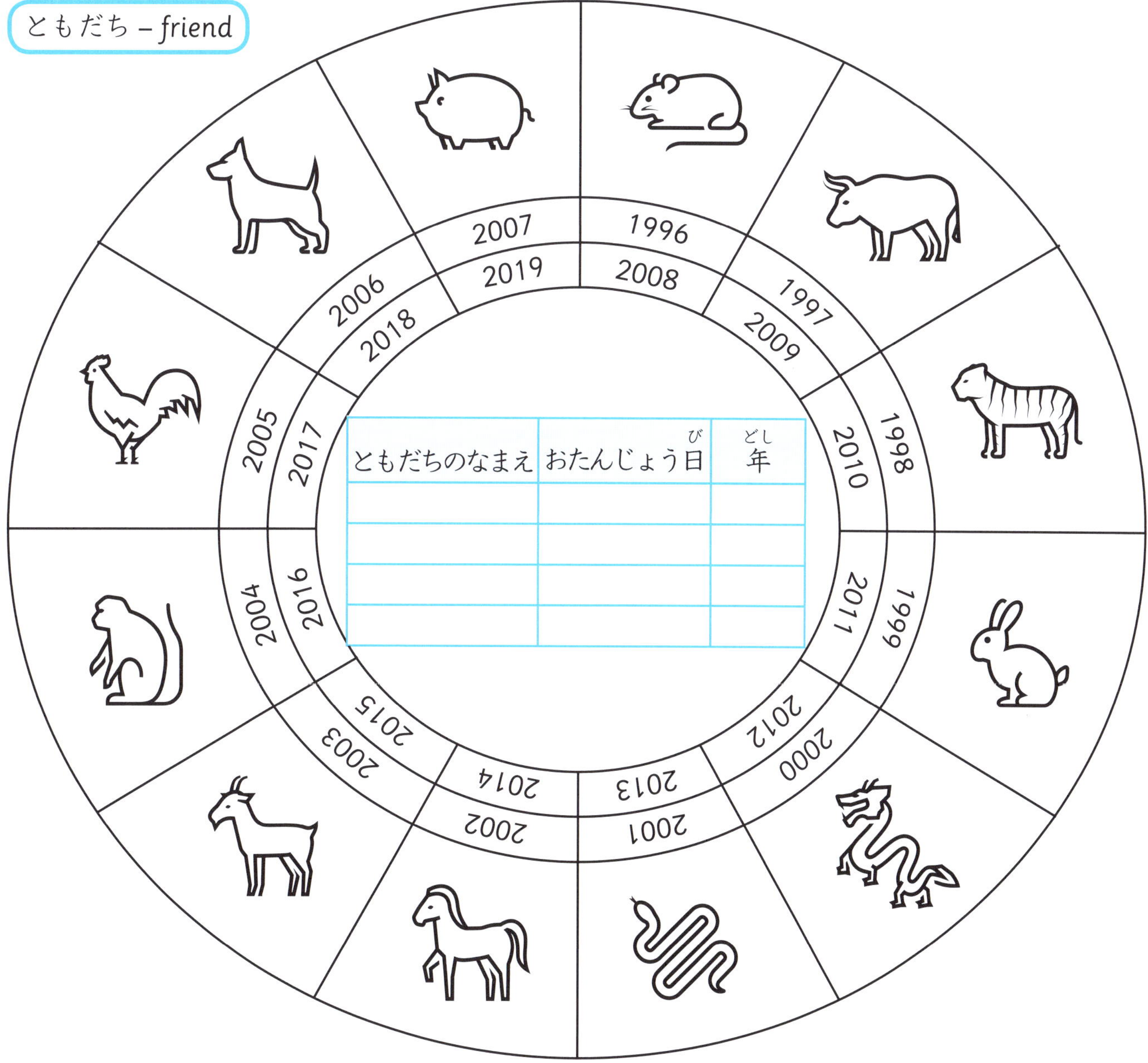

ともだちのなまえ	おたんじょう日(び)	年(どし)

Write about Tim using the information and clues given.

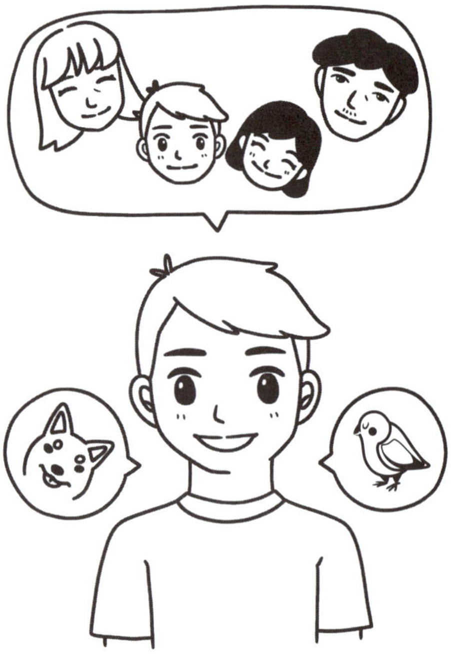

Name: Tim (ティム)
Date of birth: 20.02.05

Change the following sentences into past tense, then join each new sentence to the correct English translation. The first one has been done for you to trace over.

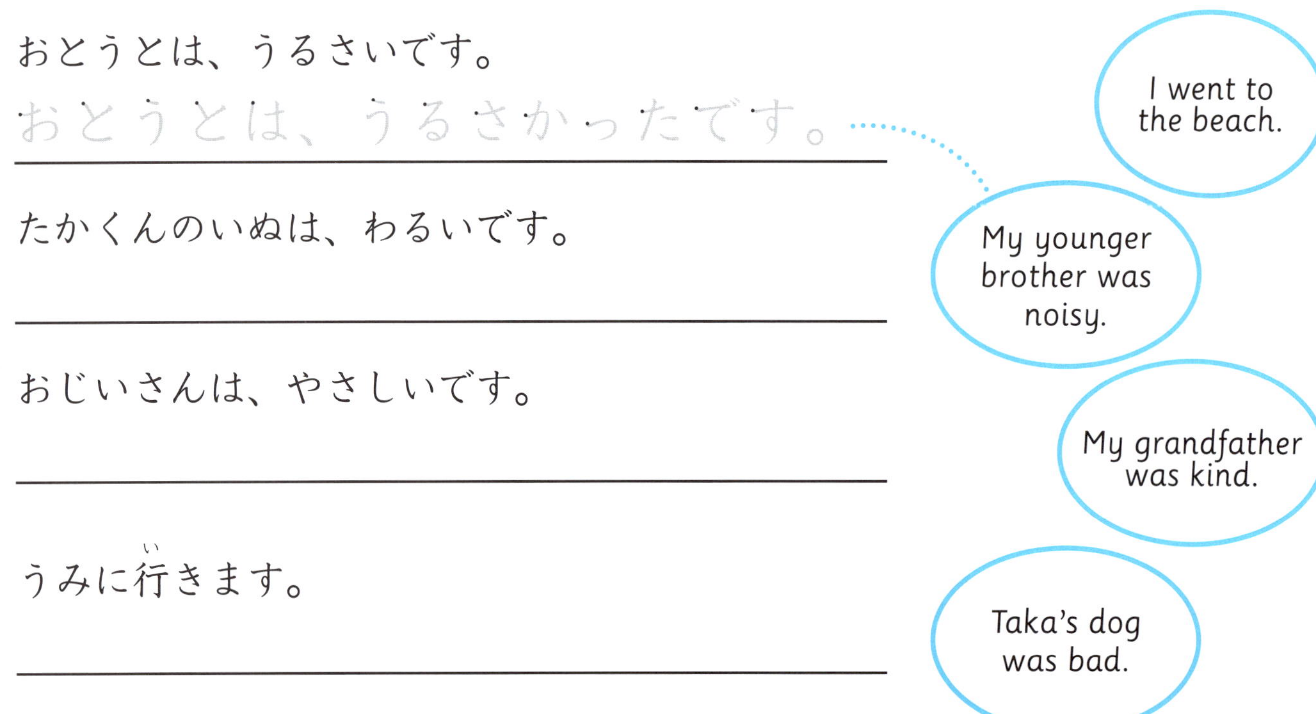

おたんじょう日(び) に 何(なに) を しましょう か。	What shall we do on your birthday?

たんじょう日(び)	に	えいが	を	見(み)ます	watch / will watch
		movie	particle O	見(み)ましょう	let's watch
		レストラン	で	たべます	(I) eat / will eat
		restaurant	particle DE	たべましょう	let's eat
(my) birthday	particle NI (on)	どうぶつえん	に	行(い)きます	(I) go / will go
		zoo	particle NI (to)	行(い)きましょう	let's go

じゃ…	ええと…	はい、そう しましょう。	いいえ、つまらない です。
Well ...	Let me see ...	Yes, let's do that.	No, it's boring.

It's almost Pipi's birthday! Look at the cartoon below showing the planning of Pipi's party. Fill in the blank boxes appropriately.

Complete the following table.

ENGLISH	JAPANESE			
	(I)do/will~	(I)do not (I) will not~	(I) did	let's~
buy				かいましょう
do/play		しません		
drink	のみます			
eat				たべましょう
go			行(い)きました	
have (family/pets)	います			
learn/study		べんきょう しません		
read				よみましょう
watch (look)	見(み)ます			

Shade the correct stroke order for the following letters.

も	ふ	ネ	木	せ
⼀ ニ も	、 丶 ふ ふ	` ラ ネ ネ	丨 十 才 木	一 七 せ
し も も	、 、 ふ ふ	` ラ ネ ネ	一 十 才 木	し 七 せ
⼀ も も	` ふ ふ ふ	フ ス ネ ネ	ノ 八 六 木	一 十 せ
Roomaji	Roomaji	Roomaji	Roomaji	Roomaji

でんわ	telephone
ばんごう	number
何(なん) ばん	what number
ゼロ	zero

でんわ ばんごう は 何(なん) ばん です か。
What is your telephone number?

☺numbers☺ の ☺numbers☺ です。
It is ☺numbers☺ ☺numbers☺ .

Ask five of your classmates for their telephone numbers, then add them to the table below. Notice the way the Japanese say の where we would leave a pause.

なまえ	でんわばんごう
ピピちゃん	9407 の 3982

Now write a sentence about each person's telephone number, like the one for Pipi below.

一 ピピちゃんのでんわばんごうは、9407 の 3982 です。

二 ____________________

三 ____________________

四 ____________________

五 ____________________

六 ____________________

Complete the sentences below by filling in the blank boxes, then collect the Japanese letters you've written and arrange them to discover Pipi's favourite place.

一 □ こにすんでいますか。

Where do you live?

二 おはよ □ ございます。

Good morning.

三 □ たとうまがすきです。

I like pigs and horses.

四 おたんじょう日(び)は、い □ ですか。

When is your birthday?

五 かぞくは、おかあさんとおね □ さんとわたしです。

My family includes my mother, my older sister and me.

六 はなさ □ は、日本人(にほんじん)です。

Hana is Japanese.

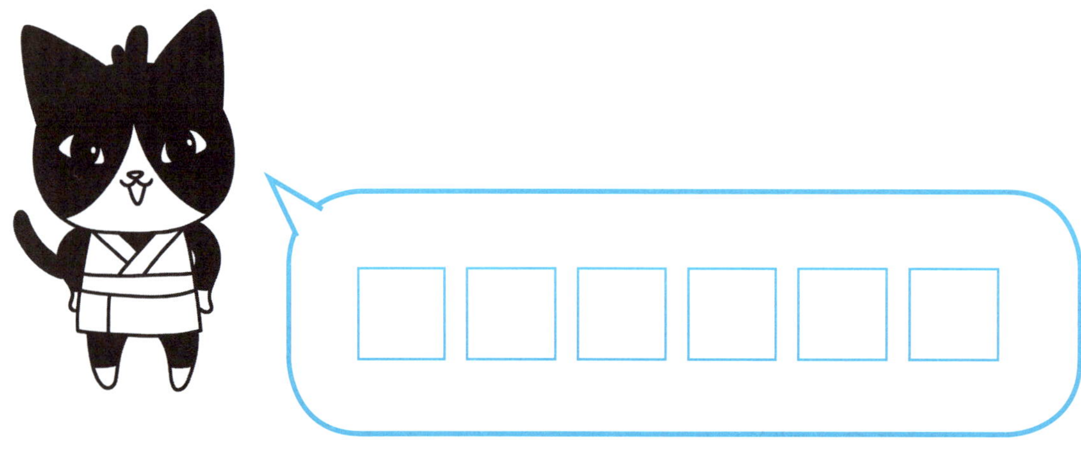

でんわ ばんごう は、何(なん) ばん です か。	What is your phone number?
☺☺☺ の ☺☺☺ です。	It's ☺☺☺ ☺☺☺.
そう です か。	Oh really?

じゃ	あとで	later	でんわ します。
	きょう	today	(I) will phone.
	こんばん	this evening	
well …	あした	tomorrow	でんわ して ください。
	らいしゅう	next week	Please phone.

The conversation below between Pipi and Hana is in the wrong order. Rewrite it in the blank speech boxes in the correct order.

そうですか
じゃ、あしたでんわします。

でんわしてください。

こんにちは。

こんにちは。

はい。でんわばんごうは、何(なん)ばんですか。

Answer the following questions using each of the answer sentences below only **once**.

一 しゅみは、何(なん)ですか。

____

二 何人(なににん)かぞくですか。

____

三 何(なん)ねんせいですか。

____

四 日本(にほん)ごがすきですか。

____

五 せんせいのなまえは、何(なん)ですか。

____

六 でんわばんごうは、何(なん)ばんですか。

____

Answer sentences

- しゅみは、おんがくです。
- たなかせんせいです。
- いいえ、つまらないです。
- 六ねんせいです。
- 9341 の 7820 です。
- 七人(しちにん)かぞくです。

月曜日(げつようび)	Monday	に
火曜日(かようび)	Tuesday	
水曜日(すいようび)	Wednesday	
木曜日(もくようび)	Thursday	
金曜日(きんようび)	Friday	particle NI (on)
土曜日(どようび)	Saturday	
日曜日(にちようび)	Sunday	
しゅうまつ	weekend	

じゃ	Well ...
もしもし	hello? (on phone)

何(なに) を しましょう か。	What shall we do?

そう です ね。	Let me see.

テニス	tennis
サッカー	soccer
クリケット	cricket
フットボール	football
コンピュータゲーム	computer games
すいえい	swimming

が	出来(でき)ます か
particle GA	can you do/play?
	出来(でき)ます
を	(I) can do/play
particle O	しましょう
	let's do/play

もしもし、ピピです。

ピピちゃん、こんにちは。

こんにちは、しゅうまつに何(なに)をしましょうか。

そうですね。テニスが出来(でき)ますか。

はい、出来(でき)ます。

じゃ、テニスをしましょう。

Write a similar dialogue for you and a friend. Draw yourself and your friend, then write your dialogue in the blank speech bubbles.

Join the correct sentence beginnings and endings with a line.

かぞくは、おじいさんと	二人(ふたり)います。
水曜日(すいようび)にがっこうに	バニです。
いもうとが	すんでいます。
月曜日(げつようび)	行(い)きます。
うさぎの なまえは	おかあさんと ぼくです。
きゅうしゅうに	せいです。
やきゅうが	うるさいです。
六ねん	出来(でき)ますか。
とりは、	ペットですか。
ペットが	いますか。
どんな	にうみに 行(い)きます。

Now cross out the English sentences below if they match the completed sentences above. Which sentence is left over?

- I'm in grade 6.
- Can you play basketball?
- Do you have a pet?
- I have two younger sisters.
- I love Japanese.
- The rabbit's name is Bunny.
- On Wednesday, I go to school.
- I live in Kyushu.
- What kind of pet is it?
- Birds are noisy.
- My family includes my grandfather, mother and me.
- On Monday, I will go to the beach.

The leftover sentence is:

Japanese: ______________________________

English: ______________________________

ぼく♂	は	スポーツ	sport	が	出来(でき)ます か
I		じゅうどう	judo		can you do?
わたし♀		テニス	tennis		出来(でき)ます
I		すいえい	swimming		can do
☺name☺くん	particle WA	バレエ	ballet	particle GA	すこし 出来(でき)ます
name♂		えいご	English		a little can do
☺name☺ さん		日本(にほん)ご	Japanese		出来(でき)ません
name♀		フランスご	French		cannot do
					ぜんぜん 出来(でき)ません
					at all cannot do

Unjumble the sentences, then assign each to the corresponding image below.

は　、　くん　じゅうどう　。　出来(でき)ます　トム　が

が　さん　。　バレエ　出来(でき)ます。　はな　すこし　、　は

出来(でき)ます　が　。　たか　は、　日本(にほん)ご　くん

は　テニス　、　ぜんぜん　ピピ　出来(でき)ません　ちゃん　が

Choose five classmates and write a sentence for each of them saying something they can do. There is one about Pipi for you to use as a model.

ピピちゃんは、フランスごが出来(でき)ます。

一 ______________________________

二 ______________________________

三 ______________________________

四 ______________________________

五 ______________________________

Using lines, join the half words to make a whole, then connect each word with its English match.

すい	ます	swimming
でき	どう	family
じゅう	しょう	judo
しま	ぞく	can do
か	しゅう	next week
らい	えい	let's do

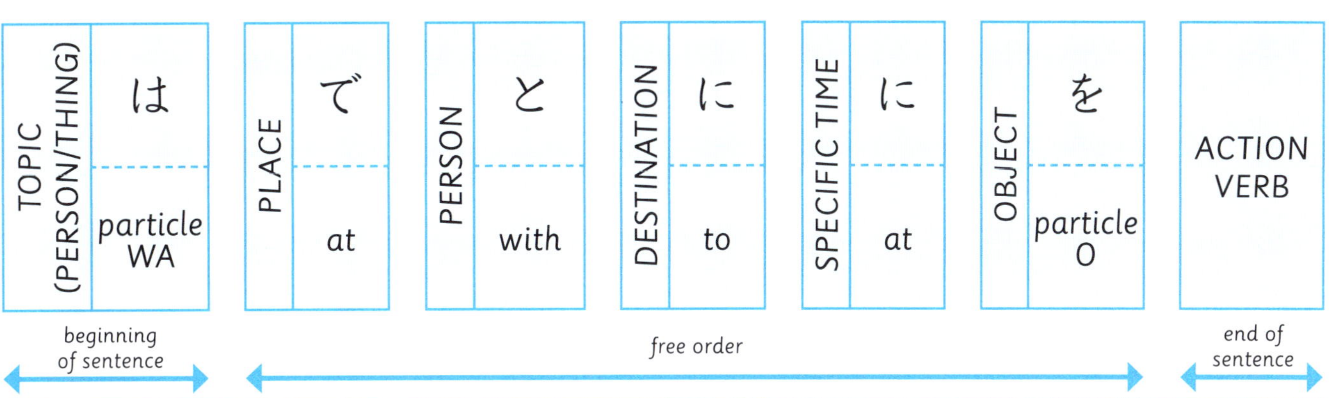

There are two important rules to remember when constructing long action sentences in Japanese. Cross out the incorrect words in the underlined pairs of words in the following rules.

1 The topic is followed/preceded by particle WA (は) and is located at the beginning/end of Japanese sentences.

2 Verbs go at the beginning/end of Japanese sentences.

ピピちゃんは、おおきいがっこうでやさしいせんせいと火曜日(かようび)におもしろい日本(にほん)ごといいスポーツをべんきょうしました。

Can you write a long sentence like the one above? Write your own sentence below, then translate it into English. Use adjectives to make a really long sentence.

Japanese ______________________________

____

English ______________________________

____

Now write your sentence in the shape of a Japanese character in the blank box, like Pipi's sentence below.

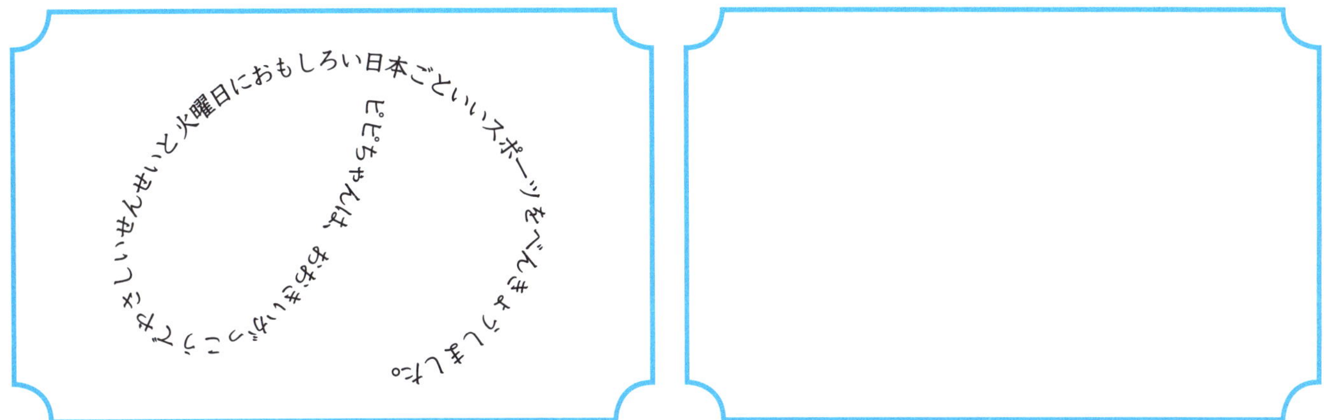

How many points can you get in just one sentence? Score your sentences using the following point system.

ordinary words:	2 points
particles:	2 points
katakana words:	3 points
adjectives:	4 points
kanji:	5 points

Sentence 1

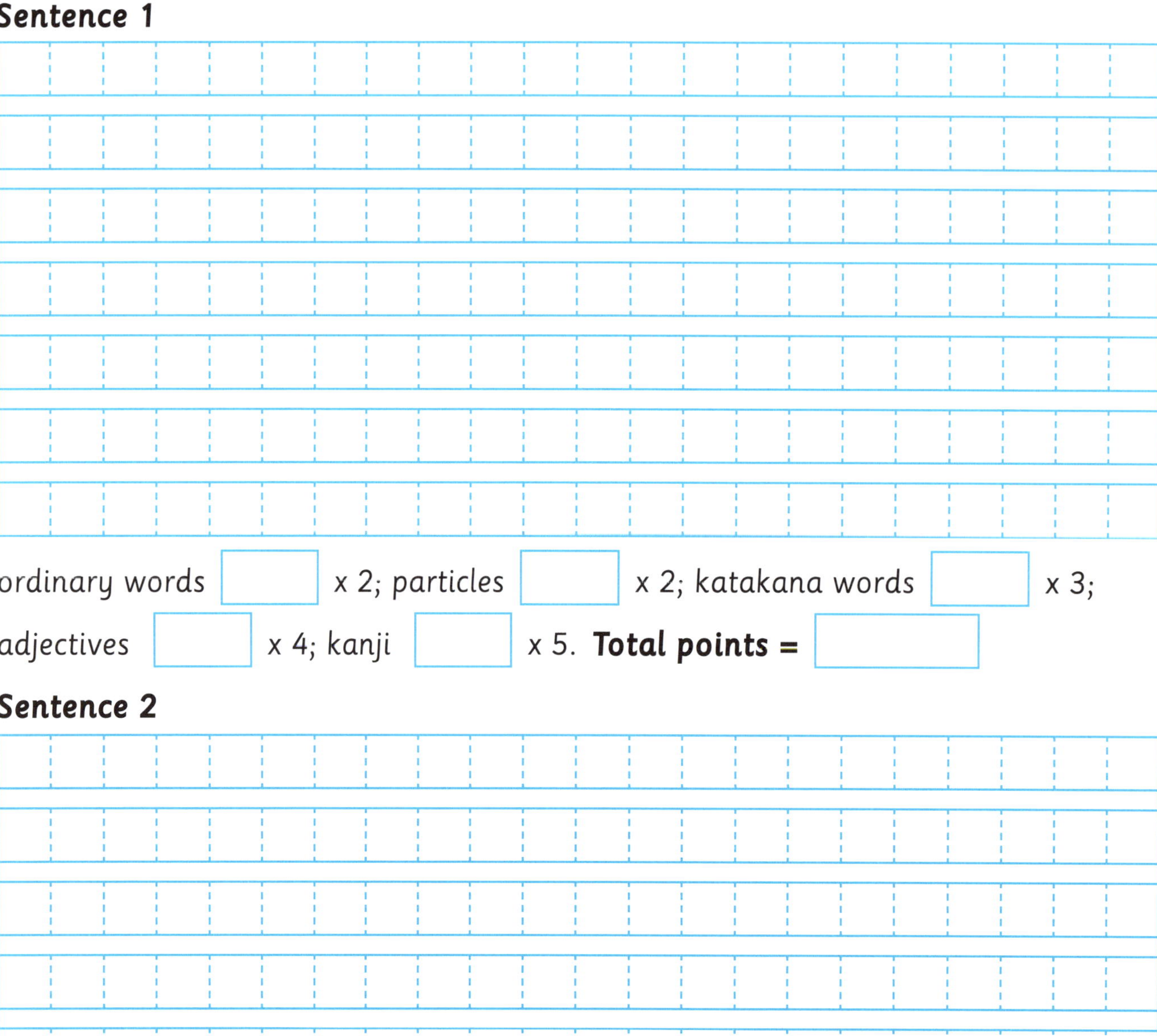

ordinary words ☐ x 2; particles ☐ x 2; katakana words ☐ x 3;
adjectives ☐ x 4; kanji ☐ x 5. **Total points =** ☐

Sentence 2

ordinary words ☐ x 2; particles ☐ x 2; katakana words ☐ x 3;
adjectives ☐ x 4; kanji ☐ x 5. **Total points =** ☐

KANJI	STROKE ORDER	くん READING		おん READING		MEANING
一		ひとり 一人	one person	いち 一	one	one
		ついたち 一日	first day of month	いちがつ 一月	January	
二		ふたり 二人	two people	に 二	two	two
		ふつか 二日	second day of month	にがつ 二月	February	
三		みっか 三日	third day of month	ざん 三	three	three
				さんにん 三人	three people	
				さんがつ 三月	March	
四		よん 四	four	し 四	four	four
		よにん 四人	four people	しがつ 四月	April	
		よっか 四日	fourth day of month			
五		いつか 五日	fifth day of month	ご 五	five	five
				ごにん 五人	five people	
				ごがつ 五月	May	

Fill in the missing information in Pipi's speech bubble. Ask your teacher for help if you need it.

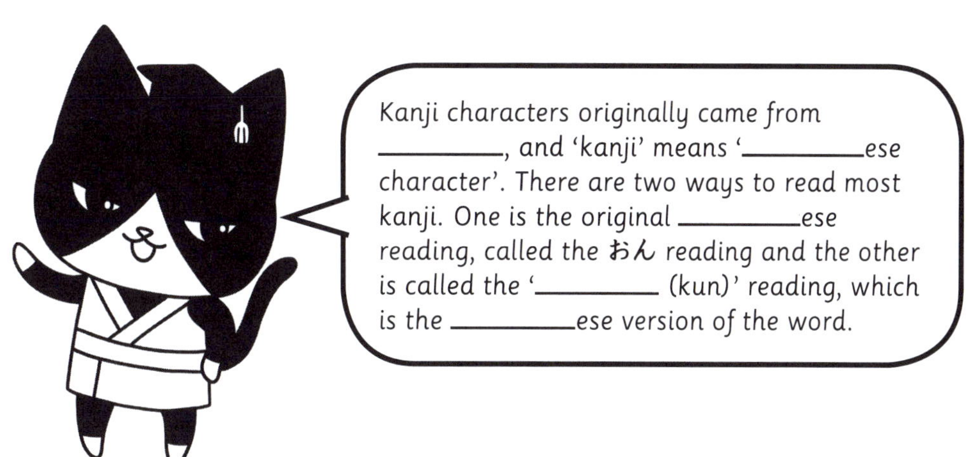

Fill in the missing furigana for the following kanji, then shade the correct English translation underneath.

Furigana are the very small letters above kanji that tell us how to read the kanji correctly. When you write vertically in Japanese, the furigana are written vertically on the right-hand side of the kanji.

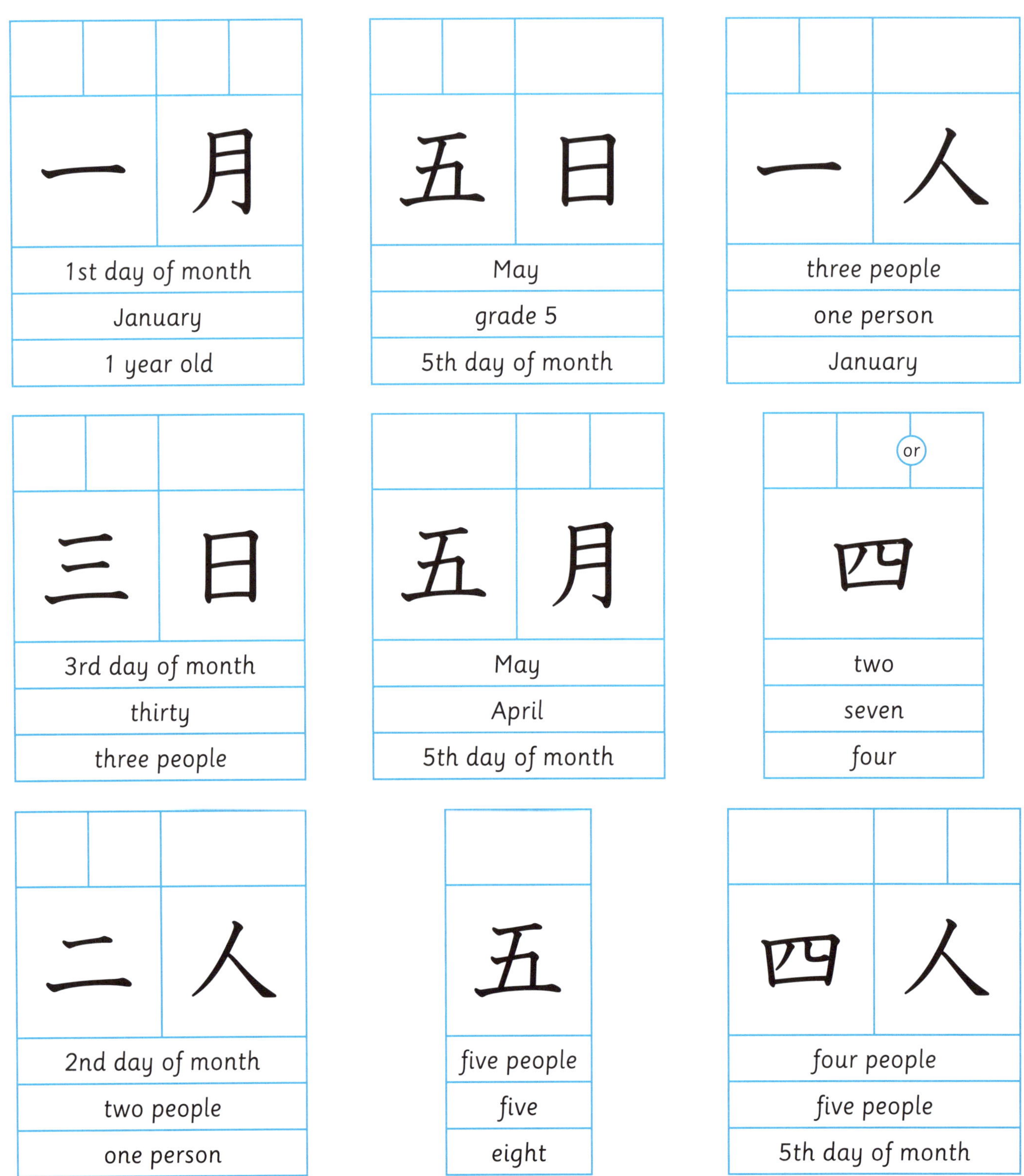

KANJI	STROKE ORDER	くん READING		おん READING		MEANING
六		むいか 六日	sixth day of month	ろく 六	six	six
				ろくにん 六人	six people	
				ろくがつ 六月	June	
七		なな 七	seven	しち 七	seven	seven
				しちにん 七人	seven people	
		なのか 七日	seventh day of month	しちがつ 七月	July	
八		ようか 八日	eighth day of month	はち 八	eight	eight
				はちにん 八人	eight people	
				はちがつ 八月	August	
九		ここのか 九日	ninth day of month	きゅう／く 九	nine	nine
				きゅうにん 九人	nine people	
				くがつ 九月	September	
				きゅう 九しゅう	Kyushu	
十		とおか 十日	tenth day of month	じゅう 十	ten	ten
				じゅうにん 十人	ten people	
				じゅうがつ 十月	October	

Complete the following sentences.

一 The おん reading for 九 is ______________ or ______________ .

二 The kanji 七 means ______________ in English.

三 ______________ are the small letters written above or next to kanji that tell you how the kanji should be read.

Rewrite the following sentences, changing the hiragana letters in bold to the appropriate kanji, then fill in the missing words in the matching English sentences.

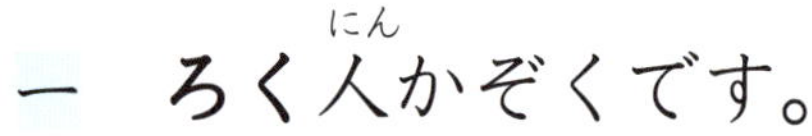

There are ______ people in my ______.

二 アイスクリームは、**よん**百円(ひゃくえん)です。

______ is 400 yen.

三 たんじょう日(び)は**しち**月(がつ)です。

My ______ is in July.

四 ぼくは、**ご**年(ねん)せいです。

I am in grade ______.

KANJI	STROKE ORDER	くん READING		おん READING		MEANING
人	ノ 人 人	あの人（ひと）	that person	三人（さんにん）	three people	person/people
				四人（よにん）	four people	
		一人（ひとり）	one person	五人（ごにん）	five people	
				六人（ろくにん）	six people	
		二人（ふたり）	two people	日本人（にほんじん）	Japanese person	
				オーストラリア人（じん）	Australian person	
				アメリカ人（じん）	American person	
大	一 ナ 大	大きい（おお）	big	大すき（だい）	like very much	big
小	亅 小 小	小さい（ちい）	small			small

Write the correct match to the English sentence in the blank box.

一 Tokyo is big.

ときょうは大きい。
とうきょうは大きです。
とうきょうは大きいです。

二 There are five people in my family.

五大かぞくです。
四人かぞくです。
五人かぞくです。

三 My younger brother is small.

いもうとは小さいです。
おとうとは小さいです。
おとうと小です。

四 My mother is Japanese.

おかあさんは日本人です。
おとうさんは日本人です。
おかあさんは日本小です。

KANJI	STROKE ORDER	くん READING	おん READING		MEANING
百			ひゃく 百	100	hundred
			にひゃく 二百	200	
			さんびゃく 三百	300	
			よんひゃく 四百	400	
			ごひゃく 五百	500	
			ろっぴゃく 六百	600	
			ななひゃく 七百	700	
			はっぴゃく 八百	800	
			きゅうひゃく 九百	900	
千			いっせん 一千	1000	thousand
			にせん 二千	2000	
			さんぜん 三千	3000	
			よんせん 四千	4000	
			ごせん 五千	5000	
			ろくせん 六千	6000	
			ななせん 七千	7000	
			はっせん 八千	8000	
			きゅうせん 九千	9000	

Put the following numbers in the correct order, from smallest to largest.

五百　六　九十三　三千　四百六十　四百　三千二百

______ ______ ______ ______ ______ ______ ______

Join the matching Japanese and English numbers to discover Pipi's favourite number.

2026 二千二十六 5000 9

九

六十四 64 340 三百四十

三千七百 3700 五千

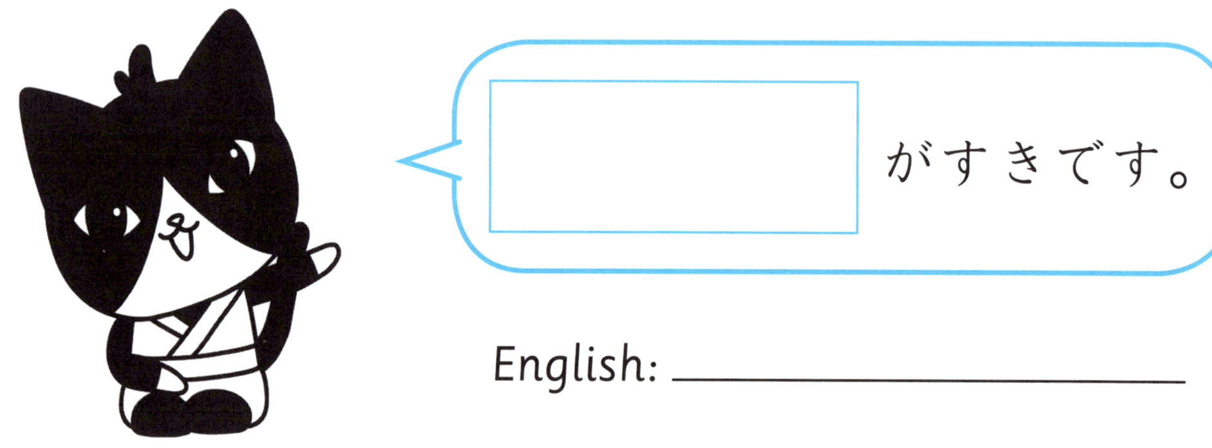

Write the numbers below in Japanese.

5000

4500

200

3762

750

400

3020

26

KANJI	STROKE ORDER	くん READING		おん READING		MEANING
日		月曜日 (げつようび)	Monday	日本 (にほん)	Japan	sun/day
		火曜日 (かようび)	Tuesday	日本人 (にほんじん)	Japanese person	
		水曜日 (すいようび)	Wednesday	日曜日 (にちようび)	Sunday	
		木曜日 (もくようび)	Thursday	まい日 (にち)	every day	
		金曜日 (きんようび)	Friday	十一日 (じゅういちにち)	11th day of month	
		土曜日 (どようび)	Saturday			
		日曜日 (にちようび)	Sunday			
		二十日 (はつか)	20th day of month			
		五日 (いつか)	5th day of month			
		たんじょう日 (び)	birthday			
		一日 (ついたち)	1st day of month			
本				本 (ほん)	book	source/book
				本しゅう (ほん)	Honshu	
				日本 (にほん)	Japan	
				日本人 (にほんじん)	Japanese person	

How many times can you write 日本 in the square below?

I wrote 日本 __________ times.

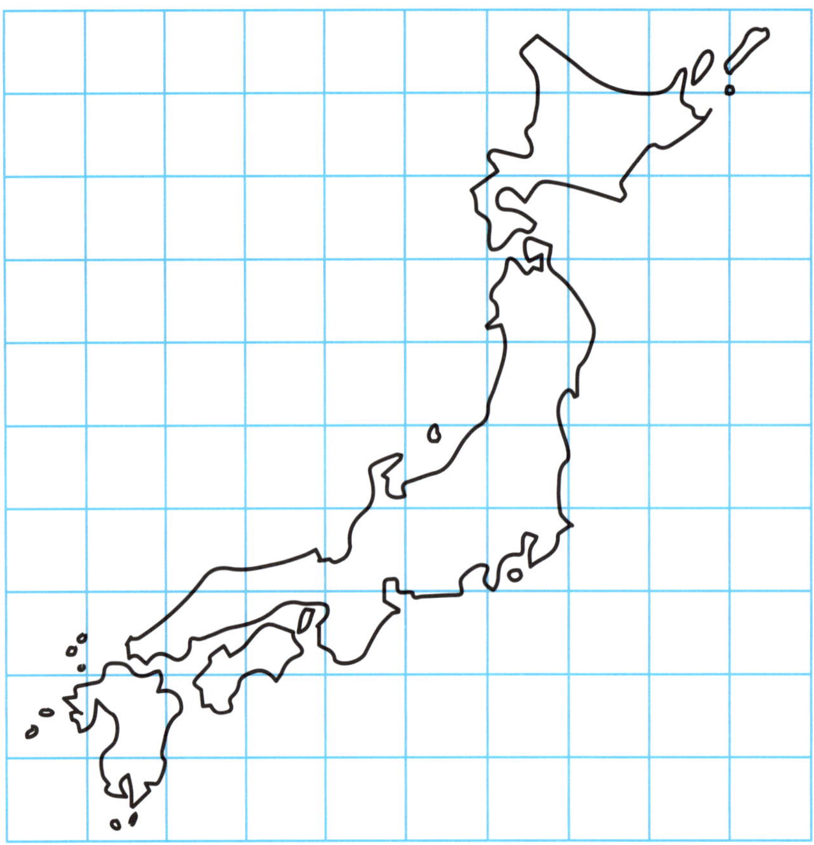

Using the image above as your guide, draw a map of Japan in the grid below, then label it with the kanji for Japan.

KANJI	STROKE ORDER	くん READING		おん READING		MEANING
何	ノ 亻 仁 仃 何 何 何	何（なに／なん）	what			what / how many
		何人（なんにん）	how many people			
		何才（なんさい）	how old			
		何（なん）ねんせい	what grade			
		何年（なにどし）	what birth year sign			
		何月（なんがつ）	what month			
円	丨 冂 円 円			十円（じゅうえん）	10 yen	yen
				百円（ひゃくえん）	100 yen	
				千円（せんえん）	1000 yen	

Write the following words in kanji.

Japan ☐☐ 300 yen ☐☐☐ June ☐☐

1st day of month ☐☐ 920 ☐☐☐☐ how many people ☐☐

Choose a partner to play noughts and crosses with, but use the kanji underneath the grid instead of noughts and crosses.

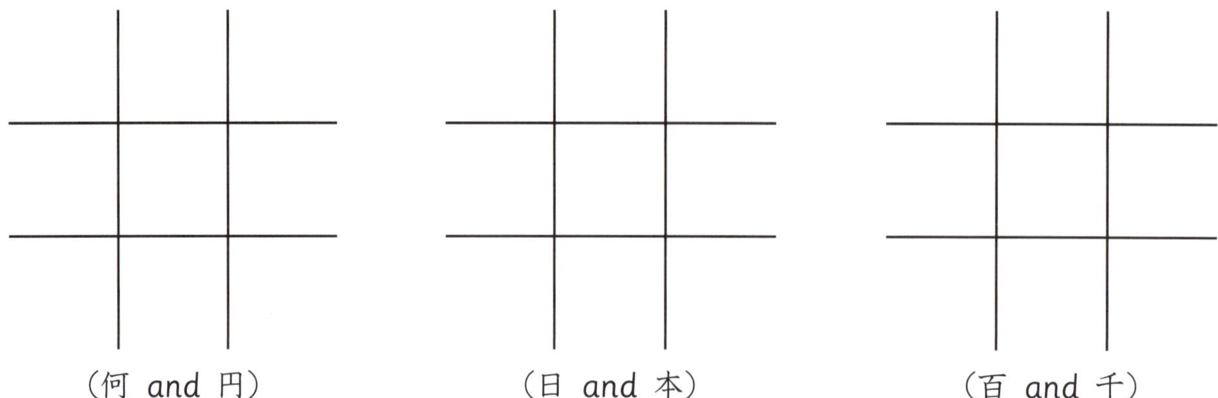

(何 and 円) (日 and 本) (百 and 千)

Now use the larger grids below. Four in a row wins!

(五 and 六) (七 and 八)

(何 and 本) (百 and 九)

KANJI	STROKE ORDER	くん READING		おん READING		MEANING
年	年	何年 (なにどし)	what birth year sign	一年せい (いちねん)	grade 1 student	year
		ねずみ年 (どし)	year of the rat	二年せい (にねん)	grade 2 student	
		うし年 (どし)	year of the cow	三年せい (さんねん)	grade 3 student	
		とら年 (どし)	year of the tiger	四年せい (よねん)	grade 4 student	
		うさぎ年 (どし)	year of the rabbit	五年せい (ごねん)	grade 5 student	
		こ年 (とし)	this year	六年せい (ろくねん)	grade 6 student	
				七年せい (ななねん)	year 7 student	
月	月	月 (つき)	moon	一月 (いちがつ)	January	moon/month
				二月 (にがつ)	February	
				三月 (さんがつ)	March	
				四月 (しがつ)	April	
				五月 (ごがつ)	May	
				六月 (ろくがつ)	June	
				七月 (しちがつ)	July	
				八月 (はちがつ)	August	
				九月 (くがつ)	September	
				十月 (じゅうがつ)	October	
				十一月 (じゅういちがつ)	November	
				十二月 (じゅうにがつ)	December	
				月曜日 (げつようび)	Monday	

In each of the following months there is one stroke missing. Fill in the missing stroke in a bold colour, then write the name of the month in English underneath.

三 ⺝

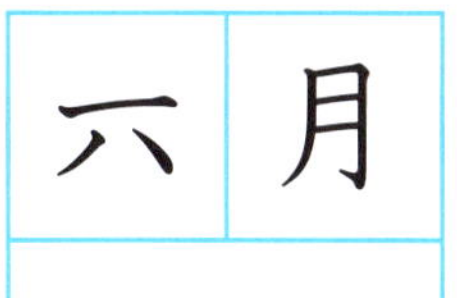

There are some furigana letters missing above the following kanji. Fill in the missing furigana letters in the shaded areas, then write the matching English underneath.

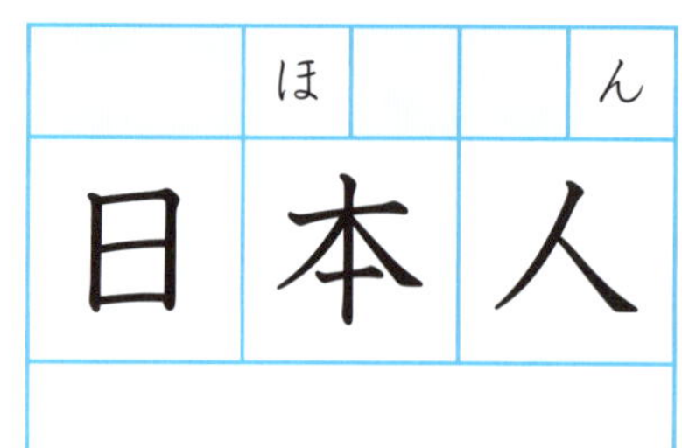

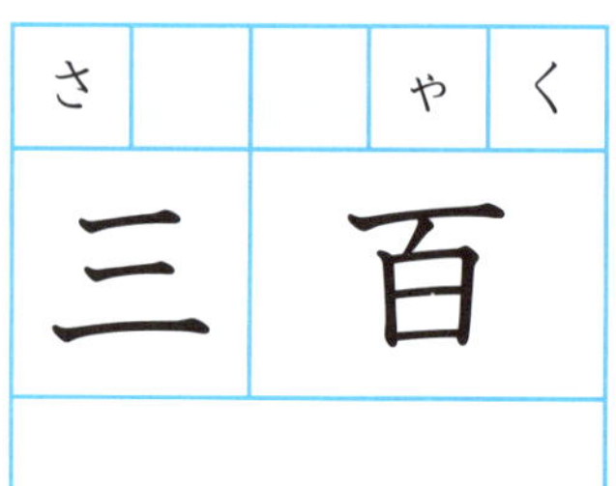

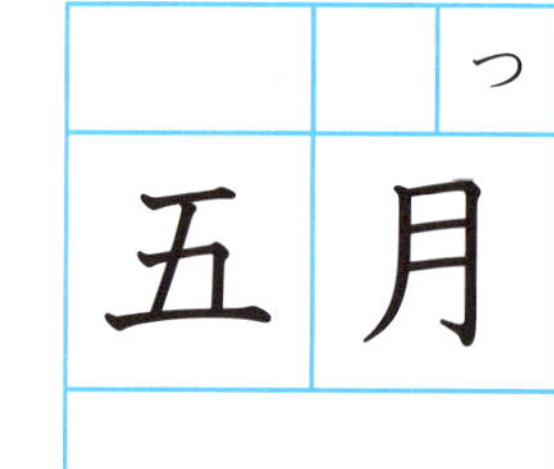

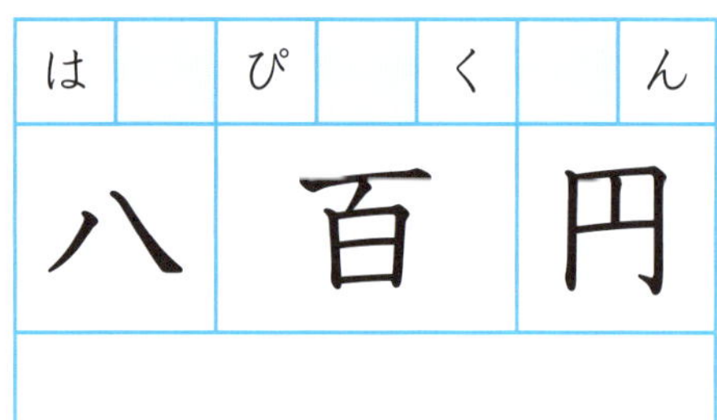

つ よ う

月曜日

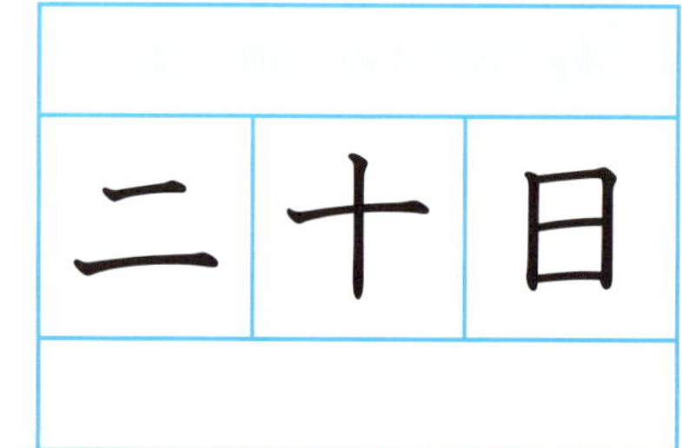

KANJI	STROKE ORDER	くん READING		おん READING		MEANING
火	丶 丶丿 ⺌ 火	火 (ひ)	fire	火曜日 (かようび)	Tuesday	fire/Tuesday
水	亅 才 才 水	水 (みず)	water	水曜日 (すいようび)	Wednesday	water/Wednesday

Circle the odd one out.

一　二十三　五百　水曜日　九千八百　三十六

二　三月　六月　十二月　五月　七月　月曜日

三　うし年　ねずみ年　二年せい　とら年　うさぎ年

Find the hidden kanji by colouring in the picture according to the following code.

日 → あか	**月** → あお	**火** → むらさき
本 → きいろ	**年** → みどり	**水** → くろ

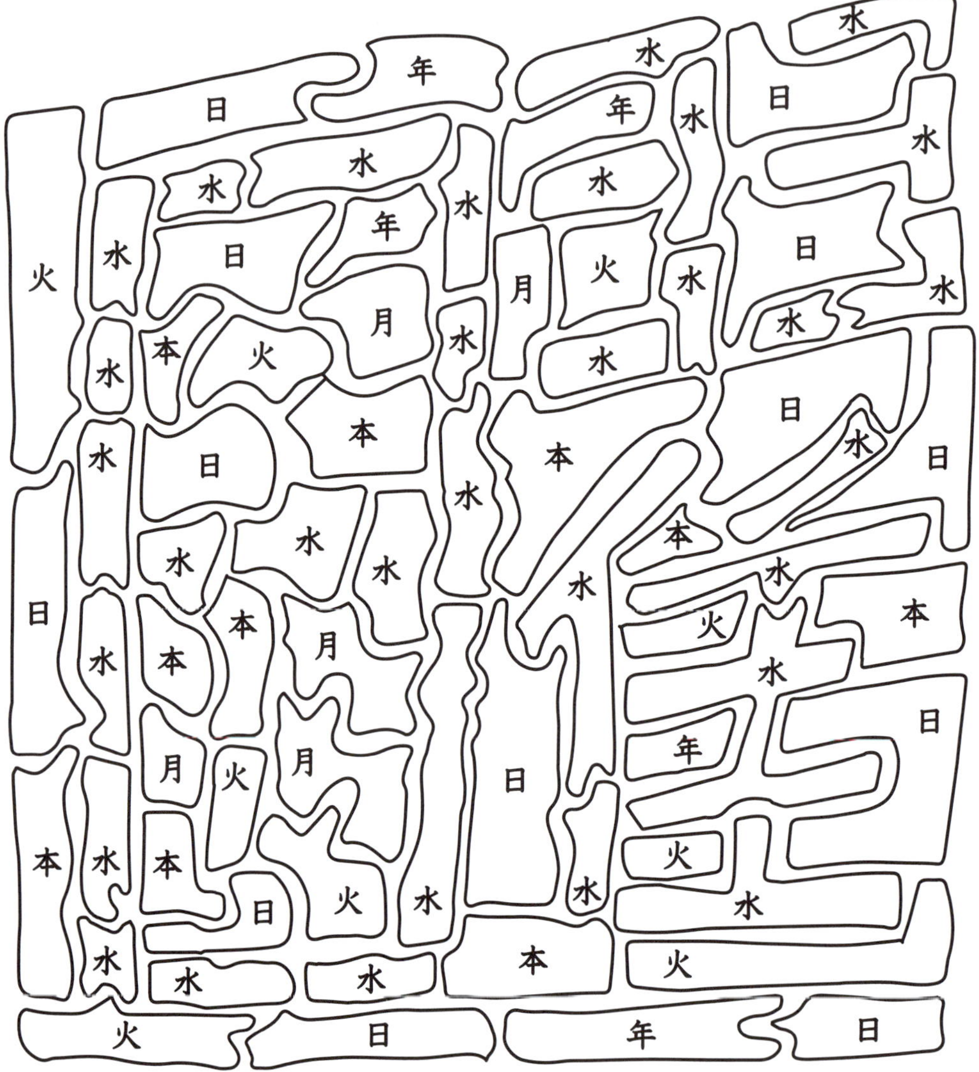

In which groups of words do you find this kanji?

KANJI	STROKE ORDER	くん READING		おん READING		MEANING
木	一 十 才 木	木（き）	tree	木曜日（もくようび）	Thursday	tree/Thursday
金	ノ 入 亼 今 全 全 余 金	お金（おかね）	money	金曜日（きんようび）	Friday	gold/money/Friday
				金（きん）	gold	
				金ぎょ（きん）	goldfish	

Circle the correct match.

Friday:	月曜日	金曜日	日本人
Thursday:	大曜日	本曜日	木曜日
big:	大きい	本きい	木きい

The following groups of words are in the wrong order. Write them in the correct order, from smallest to biggest or from first to last, in the box provided.

一 五十三 十二 三百 五 四千 三十 五十

二 十月 三月 八月 一月 十二月 六月

三 金曜日 月曜日 水曜日 火曜日 木曜日

(よう above each 曜)

四 十日 二日 五日 三十日 二十八日 四日

KANJI	STROKE ORDER	くん READING	おん READING		MEANING
土	一 十 土		土曜日 (どようび)	Saturday	Saturday
曜	丨 冂 日 ... 曜		月曜日 (げつようび)	Monday	used for days of week
			火曜日 (かようび)	Tuesday	
			水曜日 (すいようび)	Wednesday	
			木曜日 (もくようび)	Thursday	
			金曜日 (きんようび)	Friday	
			土曜日 (どようび)	Saturday	
			日曜日 (にちようび)	Sunday	

Circle the correctly written kanji.

Saturday: 月曜日 土曜月 日曜土 土曜日 十曜日

Wednesday: 火曜日 曜火日 水曜日 日水曜 金曜日

Friday: 金曜日 日曜金 日金日 木金曜 土曜日

Look at Pipi's plans for next week. There is one sentence for each day, but they are in the wrong order! Write them in the correct order, in the traditional Japanese vertical writing style.

金曜日(きんようび)にがっこうに行(い)きます。木曜日(もくようび)にすしをたべます。
水曜日(すいようび)にテニスをします。火曜日(かようび)にテレビを見(み)ます。
土曜日(どようび)に本(ほん)をよみます。日曜日(にちようび)にどうぶつえんに行(い)きます。
ピピちゃんは月曜日(げつようび)に日本(にほん)ごをべんきょうします。

Now complete Pipi's calendar by inserting the activities he has planned in the correct days.

日曜日(にちようび)	月曜日(げつようび)	火曜日(かようび)	水曜日(すいようび)	木曜日(もくようび)	金曜日(きんようび)	土曜日(どようび)

KANJI	STROKE ORDER	くん READING		おん READING	MEANING
見		見(み)ます	see		look/see
		見(み)ません	don't see		
		見(み)ました	saw		
		見(み)ませんでした	didn't see		
行		行(い)きます	go		go
		行(い)きません	don't go		
		行(い)きました	went		
		行(い)きませんでした	didn't go		

How quickly can you write the following kanji? Time yourself and write the number of seconds you took in the space provided.

KANJI	見	行	本	金	曜
YOUR KANJI					
SECONDS					

Trace over the correct kanji in the boxed pairs to make the Japanese and English sentences match.

1. I saw a book.

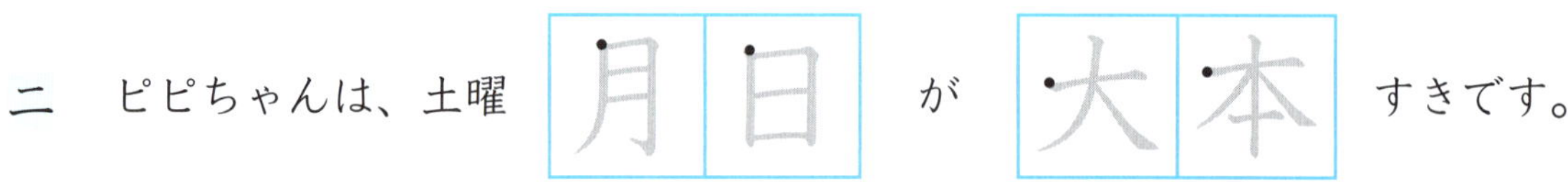

2. Pipi loves Saturday.

三　まい　| 日 | 八 |　がっこう　| に | を |　行きます。

3. I go to school every day.

四　日　| 木 | 本 |　ご がすきです。

4. I like Japanese.

五　| 大 | 本 |　しゅうは、| 木 | 大 |　きいです。

5. Honshu is big.

KANJI	STROKE ORDER	くん READING		おん READING	MEANING
出		出(で)ます	to go out		go out
		出来(でき)ます	can do		
		出来(でき)ません	can't do		
		出来(でき)ました	could do		
		出来(でき)ませんでした	couldn't do		
来		来(き)ます	to come		come
		出来(でき)ます	can do		
		出来(でき)ません	can't do		
		出来(でき)ました	could do		
		出来(でき)ませんでした	couldn't do		

Next to each activity, write either 出来(でき)ます (I can do it) or 出来(でき)ません (I can't do it).

テニス ______ 日本(にほん)ご ______

フットボール ______ じゅうどう ______

The following words have been written in mirror writing. Write each word in the correct way in the box underneath, then translate into English in the remaining box. Use a mirror if you are stuck.

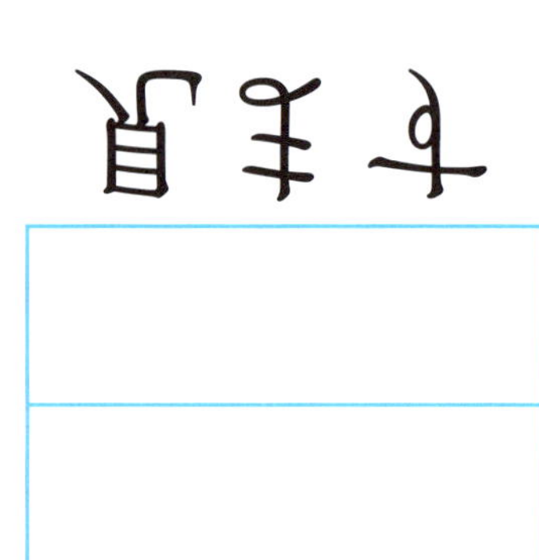

KANJI	STROKE ORDER	くん READING		おん READING	MEANING
夏		夏（なつ）	summer		summer
秋		秋（あき）	autumn		autumn

Complete the following kanji.

autumn

book

100

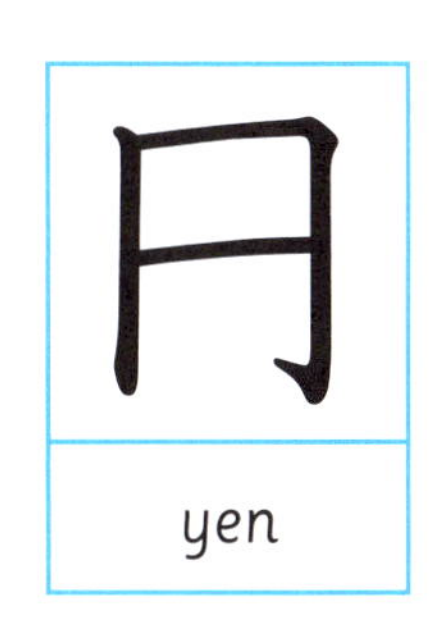

yen

what

Hina has written the kanji for summer using Japanese numbers from 1 to 42.

Using the same system, write the kanji for autumn. You may use numbers in order, or the days of the week in order. (Repeat the seven days as many times as you need to.)

KANJI	STROKE ORDER	くん READING		おん READING	MEANING
冬	ノ ク 夂 冬 冬 冬 冬 冬 冬	冬（ふゆ）	winter		winter
春	一 二 三 声 夫 夫 春 春 春 春 春 春	春（はる）	spring		spring

How many strokes are there in the following kanji? Translate each kanji into English.

本	
kanji	strokes
English	

夏	
kanji	strokes
English	

冬	
kanji	strokes
English	

火	
kanji	strokes
English	

Do you remember the season song? It is written underneath in roomaji. Rewrite it using hiragana letters and kanji where appropriate, then decorate your song.

natsu wa, atsui desu.

aki wa, suzushii desu.

fuyu wa, samui desu.

haru wa, atatakai desu.

How would you write the season song in English?

English: ______________________________

____

____

____

Choose nine items from the following list, then write one item in each bingo square. Listen to your teacher to play the game.

じこしょうかい	self introduction	一人	one person	三十	30
五人かぞくです。	There are five people in my family.	二人	two people	四十五	45
何人かぞくですか。	How many people in your family?	四人	four people	七	7
おじさんがいますか。	Do you have an uncle?	十人	ten people	二十八	28
いもうとが二人います。	I have two younger sisters.	かぞく	family	九十一	91
おとうとはいません。	I have no younger brother.	おかあさん	mother	八十	80
おにいさんは、やさしいです。	My big brother is kind.	おにいさん	older brother	四	4
おとうさんは、うるさいです。	My dad is noisy.	おじさん	uncle	二十六	26
いもうとは、わるいです。	My little sister is bad.	おばさん	aunt	五十	50

LANGUAGE LESSON BINGO		

Choose nine letters, letter groups, or letter blends from the following list, then write one item in each bingo square. Listen to your teacher to play the game.

WRITING LESSON BINGO		

一	1	五人	5 people
二	2	六人	6 people
三	3	大きい	big
四	4	小さい	small
五	5	百	100
六	6	二百	200
七	7	三百	300
八	8	四百	400
九	9	千	1000
十	10	五千	5000
一人	1 person	六千	6000
二人	2 people	七千	7000
三人	3 people	八千	8000
四人	4 people		

Choose nine items from the following list, then write one item in each bingo square. Listen to your teacher to play the game.

おばあさんがいます。	I have a grandmother.	いもうと	little sister	ねこ	cat
ペットがいますか。	Do you have a pet?	おとうと	little brother	八十九	89
ぼくのペットは、とりです。	My pet is a bird.	あひる	duck	二百	200
へびのなまえはサイモンです。	The snake's name is Simon.	きんぎょ	goldfish	七千	7000
あひるはだれのペットですか。	Whose pet is the duck?	へび	snake	五百六十	560
いぬは、はなさんのペットです。	The dog is Hana's pet.	うま	horse	六	6
どんなペットですか。	What kind of pet is it?	うさぎ	rabbit	七十四	74
かわいいうさぎです。	It's a cute rabbit.	いぬ	dog	四千三百	4300
うまは大きいです。	The horse is big.	とり	bird	十二	12

LANGUAGE LESSON BINGO		

Choose nine letters, letter groups, or letter blends from the following list, then write one item in each bingo square. Listen to your teacher to play the game.

WRITING LESSON BINGO		

まい日	every day	三月	March
一日	1st of month	四月	April
二日	2nd of month	五月	May
三日	3rd of month	六月	June
四日	4th of month	七月	July
日本	Japan	八月	Aug
本しゅう	Honshu	九月	Sept
千円	¥1000	十月	Oct
百円	¥100	十一月	Nov
何人	how many people	十二月	Dec
何さい	how old	五年せい	grade 5
何月	what month?	六年せい	grade 6
一月	Jan	何年	what year sign
二月	Feb		

Choose nine items from the following list, then write one item in each bingo square. Listen to your teacher to play the game.

おかあさんはいません。	I don't have a mother.	たんじょう日	(my) birthday	たべます	eat
うまのなまえはトマスです。	The horse's name is Thomas.	いつ	when	見ます	see
ねこは小さいです。	The cat is small.	五月一日	1st of May	行きます	go
たんじょう日は 五月です。	My birthday is in May.	六月四日	4th of June	つまらない	boring
おたんじょう日はいつですか。	When is your birthday?	八月二十日	20th of August	いい	good
何年ですか。	What birth year sign are you?	九月八日	8th of September	じゃ	well
たつ年です。	I'm the year of the dragon.	えいが	movie	ねずみ	mouse
何をしましょうか。	What shall we do?	レストラン	restaurant	うし	cow
えいがを見ましょう。	Let's watch a movie.	どうぶつえん	zoo	とら	tiger

LANGUAGE LESSON BINGO		

Choose nine letters, letter groups, or letter blends from the following list, then write one item in each bingo square. Listen to your teacher to play the game.

WRITING LESSON BINGO		

月曜日	Monday	何人	how many people?
火曜日	Tuesday		
水曜日	Wednesday	日本	Japan
木曜日	Thursday	大きい	big
金曜日	Friday	小さい	small
土曜日	Saturday	水	water
日曜日	Sunday	本	book
見ます	look	二千	2000
行きます	go	三千	3000
二月	February	四千	4000
日本人	Japanese person	五百	500
うし年	year of the cow	六百	600
こ年	this year	七百	700
百円	¥100	八百	800

Choose nine items from the following list, then write one item in each bingo square. Listen to your teacher to play the game.

六人かぞくです。	There are six people in my family.	かぞく	family	一日	1st of month
ぼくのペットはかわいいです。	My pet is cute.	でんわ	phone	二日	2nd of month
おばあさんはやさしいです。	Grandma is kind.	ばんごう	number	三日	3rd of month
おとうとのなまえはアンガスです。	My little brother's name is Angus.	何ばん	what number?	四日	4th of month
でんわばんごうは何ばんですか。	What is your phone number?	もしもし	hello (on phone)	五日	5th of month
あとででんわします。	I will phone you later.	すこし	a little	六月	June
でんわしてください。	Please phone.	出来ません	can't do	七月	July
火曜日にテニスをしましょう。	Let's play tennis on Tuesday.	しゅうまつ	weekend	八月	August
すいえいが出来ますか。	Can you swim?	きょう	today	九月	September

LANGUAGE LESSON BINGO		

Choose nine letters, letter groups, or letter blends from the following list, then write one item in each bingo square. Listen to your teacher to play the game.

WRITING LESSON BINGO		

夏	summer	一月	January
秋	autumn	二月	February
冬	winter	三月	March
春	spring	四月	April
出来ます	can do	五日	5th of month
見ます	see	何	what
行きます	go	円	yen
月曜日	Monday	日本	Japan
火曜日	Tuesday	日本人	Japanese person
水曜日	Wednesday		
木曜日	Thursday	本	book
金曜日	Friday	五千	5000
土曜日	Saturday	一日	1st of month
日曜日	Sunday	三百	300

LISTENING

Listen to the teacher, then circle the correct answer.

1	2	3	4	5
mother self introduction family	family uncle how many?	older brother younger sister	There are five people in my family. How many people are in your family? I have a younger sister.	I don't have an older brother. I don't have an older sister. I have an older sister.

6	7	8	9	10
My dad is noisy. My brother is noisy. My dad is kind.	My younger sister is bad. My mother is noisy. My uncle is kind.	aunt uncle mother	I have three younger brothers. I have no younger brothers. I have three younger sisters.	I have no younger sisters. There are four people in my family. How many people are in your family?

READING

Look at the cards the teacher will show you. Circle the correct answer.

1	2	3	4	5
いち く さん	さん に はち	ご し ろく	よんせん よんひゃく さんぜん	ひとり ふたり さんにん

6	7	8	9	10
こうさい おおさい ちいさい	しちじゅう じゅうはち はちじゅう	ななにん ふたり ろくにん	おおきい ちいきい ほんきい	ごひゃく ごぜん ごせん

CONGRATULATIONS! You remembered ______ things about Japan and its language.

LISTENING

Listen to the teacher, then circle the correct answer.

1	2	3	4	5
good kind bad	My pet is a snake. I have two pets. Do you have a pet?	dog rabbit cat	Birds are good. I like birds. I have a bird.	I have a dog. I have a bird and a cat. I have a bird and a dog.

6	7	8	9	10
horse mother aunt	I like pets. My pet is a dog. What is your pet?	what whose when	big good interesting/ funny	What kind of pet is it? Whose pet is it? What's your pet's name?

READING

Look at the cards the teacher will show you. Circle the correct answer.

1	2	3	4	5
しがつ ごがつ いつか	よんひゃく よんせん しひゃく	もくきい ちいきい おおきい	ろっぴゃくえん ごひゃくえん ろっぴゃくおん	ろくにん なんにん なんねん

6	7	8	9	10
よねんせい ごにんせい ごねんせい	じゅうがつ じゅうげつ はちがつ	ほん にほん にちほん	ねずみどし ねずみねん ねずみとし	ついたち いつか むいか

CONGRATULATIONS! You remembered ______ things about Japan and its language.

HOW MUCH CAN YOU REMEMBER? LL 1 – 15; WL 1 – 11

LISTENING

Listen to the teacher, then circle the correct answer.

1	2	3	4	5
what what kind of whose	older sister interesting/funny cute	February July August	When is your birthday? My birthday is in March. My birthday is in May.	4th of March 9th of March 2nd of March

6	7	8	9	10
17th of April 24th of April 30th of April	How are you? 29th of June What is your year sign?	year of the monkey year of the dragon year of the mouse/rat	What shall we do? What birth year sign are you? Let's go to the zoo.	Let's eat. Let's watch. Let's go.

READING

Look at the cards the teacher will show you. Circle the correct answer.

1	2	3	4	5
なんさい なんねんせい いつさい	とらどし とらとし とらねん	すようび とようび すいようび	はちがつ しがつ はちげつ	まず みず おちゃ

6	7	8	9	10
かようび げつようび すいようび	びようか とようび かようび	きんようび もくようび きんようにち	たびます いきます みます	よきます みきます いきます

CONGRATULATIONS! You remembered ______ things about Japan and its language.

LISTENING

Listen to the teacher, then circle the correct answer.

1	2	3	4	5
school restaurant movie	I eat. Let's eat. Let's go.	Let's watch. Let's go. Let's do that.	Let's watch TV. Let's go to the zoo. Let's eat at a restaurant.	What is your telephone number? My telephone number is 532 976. I like talking on the phone.

6	7	8	9	10
cute interesting/ funny boring	832 487 652 731 651 827	late today this evening	Let's phone. Please phone. Please go.	I can play tennis. Shall we play tennis? I like tennis.

READING

Look at the cards the teacher will show you. Circle the correct answer.

1	2	3	4	5
はっぽん にしん にほん	すいようび みかようび もくようび	かようび どようび もくようび	いきます しきます やきます	できます します みます

6	7	8	9	10
よる はる ひる	ひろ ふゆ なつ	あき なつ ふゆ	あき にた なつ	いきます たべます できます

CONGRATULATIONS! You remembered ____ things about Japan and its language.

WORDLIST

WORDLIST – ENGLISH/JAPANESE	
ENGLISH	JAPANESE/ROOMAJI
1 · one	一 / いち I CHI
1 o'clock	一じ / いちじ I CHI JI
1 person	一人 / ひとり HI TO RI
1st (day)	一日 / ついたち TSU I TA CHI
10 · ten	十 / じゅう JU U
10 o'clock	十じ / じゅうじ JU U JI
10 people	十人 / じゅうにん JU U NI N
10th (day)	十日 / とおか TO O KA
100 · one hundred	百 / ひゃく HYA KU
1000	千 / 一千 / せん / いっせん SE N / I S SE N
11 · eleven	十一 / じゅう いち JU U I CHI
11 o'clock	十一じ / じゅういちじ JU U I CHI JI
11th (day)	十一日 / じゅういちにち JU U I CHI NI CHI
12th (day)	十二日 / じゅうににち JU U NI NI CHI
12 · twelve	十二 / じゅう に JU U NI
12 o'clock	十二じ / じゅうにじ JU U NI JI
13th (day)	十三日 / じゅうさんにち JU U SA N NI CHI
13 · thirteen	十三 / じゅう さん JU U SA N
14th (day)	十四日 / じゅうよっか JU U YO K KA
14 · fourteen	十四 / じゅう し / よん JU U SHI / YO N
15th (day)	十五日 / じゅうごにち JU U GO NI CHI
15 · fifteen	十五 / じゅう ご JU U GO
16th (day)	十六日 / じゅうろくにち JU U RO KU NI CHI
16 · sixteen	十六 / じゅう ろく JU U RO KU
17th (day)	十七日 / じゅうしちにち JU U SHI CHI NI CHI
17 · seventeen	十七 / じゅう しち / なな JU U SHI CHI / NA NA
18th (day)	十八日 / じゅうはちにち JU U HA CHI NI CHI
18 · eighteen	十八 / じゅう はち JU U HA CHI
19th (day)	十九日 / じゅうくにち JU U KU NI CHI
19 · nineteen	十九 / じゅう く / きゅう JU U KU / KYU U
2 · two	二 / に NI
2nd (day)	二日 / ふつか FU TSU KA
2 o'clock	二じ / にじ NI JI
2 people	二人 / ふたり FU TA RI
20th (day)	二十日 / はつか HA TSU KA
20 · twenty	二十 / にじゅう NI JU U
200	二百 / にひゃく NI HYA KU
2000	二千 / にせん NI SE N
21st (day)	二十一日 / にじゅう いちにち NI JU U I CHI NI CHI
21 · twenty-one	二十一 / にじゅういち NI JU U I CHI

WORDLIST – ENGLISH/JAPANESE	
ENGLISH	JAPANESE/ROOMAJI
22nd (day)	二十二日 / にじゅうににち NI JU U NI NI CHI
23rd (day)	二十三日 / にじゅうさんにち NI JU U SA N NI CHI
24th (day)	二十四日 / にじゅうよっか NI JU U YO K KA
25th (day)	二十五日 / にじゅうごにち NI JU U GO NI CHI
26th (day)	二十六日 / にじゅうろくにち NI JU U RO KU NI CHI
27th (day)	二十七日 / にじゅうしちにち NI JU U SHI CHI NI CHI
28th (day)	二十八日 / にじゅうはちにち NI JU U HA CHI NI CHI
29th (day)	二十九日 / にじゅうくにち NI JU U KU NI CHI
3 · three	三 / さん SA N
3 o'clock	三じ / さんじ SA N JI
3 people	三人 / さんにん SA N NI N
3rd (day)	三日 / みっか MI K KA
30th (day)	三十日 / さんじゅうにち SA N JU U NI CHI
30 · thirty	三十 / さんじゅう SA N JU U
300	三百 / さんびゃく SA N BYA KU
3000	三千 / さんぜん SA N ZE N
31st (day)	三十一日 / さんじゅういちにち SA N JU U I CHI NI CHI
4 · four	四 / し / よん SHI / YO N
4 o'clock	四じ / よじ YO JI
4 people	四人 / よにん YO NI N
4th (day)	四日 / よっか YO K KA
40 · forty	四十 / よんじゅう YO N JU U
400	四百 / よんひゃく YO N HYA KU
4000	四千 / よんせん YO N SE N
5 · five	五 / ご GO
5 o'clock	五じ / ごじ GO JI
5 people	五人 / ごにん GO NI N
5th (day)	五日 / いつか ITS U KA
50 · fifty	五十 / ご じゅう GO JU U
500	五百 / ごひゃく GO HYA KU
5000	五千 / ごせん GO SE N
6 · six	六 / ろく RO KU
6 o'clock	六じ / ろくじ RO KU JI
6 people	六人 / ろくにん RO KU NI N
6th (day)	六日 / むいか MU I KA
60 · sixty	六十 / ろくじゅう RO KU JU U
600	六百 / ろっぴゃく RO P PYA KU
6000	六千 / ろくせん RO KU SE N
7 · seven	七 / しち / なな SHI CHI / NA NA
7 o'clock	七じ / しちじ SHI CHI JI

WORDLIST – ENGLISH/JAPANESE	
ENGLISH	JAPANESE/ROOMAJI
7 people	七人 / しちにん RO KU NI N
7th (day)	七日 / なのか NA NO KA
70 · seventy	七十 / しち / ななじゅう SHI CHI / NA NA JU U
700	七百 / ななひゃく NA NA HYA KU
7000	七千 / ななせん NA NA SE N
8 · eight	八 / はち HA CHI
8 o'clock	八じ / はちじ HA CHI JI
8 people	八人 / はちにん HA CHI NI N
8th (day)	八日 / ようか YO O KA
80 · eighty	八十 / はちじゅう HA CHI JU U
800	八百 / はっぴゃく HA P PYA KU
8000	八千 / はっせん HA S SE N
9 · nine	九 / く / きゅう KU / KYU U
9 o'clock	九じ / くじ KU JI
9 people	九人 / きゅうにん KYU U NI N
9th (day)	九日 / ここのか KO KO NO KA
90 · ninety	九十 / きゅうじゅう KYU U JU U
900	九百 / きゅうひゃく KYU U HYA KU
9000	九千 / きゅうせん KYU U SE N
Africa	アフリカ A FU RI KA
am/is/are	です DE SU
America	アメリカ A ME RI KA
American	アメリカ人 / アメリカじん A ME RI KA JI N
and	と TO
and also/then	そして SO SHI TE
April	四がつ / しがつ SHI GA TSU
Asia	アジア A JI A
at (a time)	に NI
at all	ぜんぜん ZE N ZE N
ate	たべました TA BE MA SHI TA
August	八がつ / はちがつ HA CHI GA TSU
aunt	おばさん O BA SA N
Australia	オーストラリア O O SU TO RA RI A
Australian (person)	オーストラリア人 / オーストラリアじん O O SU TO RA RI A JI N
autumn	秋 / あき A KI
bad	わるい WA RU I
ballet	バレエ BA RE E
baseball	やきゅう YA KYU U
basketball	バスケットボール BA SU KE T TO BO O RU
beach/sea	うみ U MI
bicycle	じてんしゃ JI TE N SHA

WORDLIST – ENGLISH/JAPANESE	
ENGLISH	JAPANESE/ROOMAJI
big	おおきい O O KI I
bird	とり TO RI
(my) birthday	たんじょうび TA N YO O BI
(your) birthday	おたんじょうび O TA N YO O BI
black	くろ KU RO
blue	あお A O
book	ほん HO N
boring	つまらない TSU MA RA NA I
bought	かいました KA I MA SHI TA
brother (older)	おにいさん O NI I SA N
brother (younger)	おとうと O TO O TO
brown	ちゃいろ CHA I RO
bus	バス BA SU
buy	かいます KA I MA SU
by (transport)	で DE
can do/play	出来ます / できます DE KI MA SU
can you do/play?	出来ますか / できますか DE KI MA SU KA
cannot do	出来ません / できません DE KI MA SE N
Canada	カナダ KA NA DA
Canadian (person)	カナダ人 / カナダじん KA NA DA JI N
car	くるま KU RU MA
cartoon, comic	まんが MA N GA
cat	ねこ NE KO
cow	うし U SHI
CD	CD SHII DII
China	ちゅうごく CHU U GO KU
Chinese (person)	ちゅうごく人 / ちゅうごくじん CHU U GO KU JI N
cinema	えいがかん E I GA KA N
coffee	コーヒー KO O HI I
cold	さむい SA MU I
computer games	コンピュータゲーム KO N PYU U TA GE E MU
cool	すずしい SU ZU SHI I
cricket	クリケット KU RI KE T TO
December	十二がつ / じゅうにがつ JU U NI GA TSU
department store	デパート DE PA A TO
did	しました SHI MA SHI TA
didn't go	行きませんでした / いきませんでした I KI MA SE N DE SHI TA
do not go	行きません / いきません I KI MA SE N
do/play	します SHI MA SU
dog	いぬ I NU
don't buy	かいません KA I MA SE N

WORDLIST – ENGLISH/JAPANESE	
ENGLISH	JAPANESE/ROOMAJI
don't play/do	しません SHI MA SE N
dragon	たつ TA TSU
drank	のみました NO MI MA SHI TA
drink	のみます NO MI MA SU
duck	あひる A HI RU
eat	たべます TA BE MA SU
England	イギリス I GI RI SU
English (language)	えいご E I GO
English (person)	イギリス人 / イギリスじん I GI RI SU JI N
Europe	ヨーロッパ YO O RO P PA
every day	まい日 / まいにち MA I NI CHI
Excuse me, but ...	すみませんが… SU MI MA SE N GA
Excuse me.	すみません。 SU MI MA SE N
eye(s)	め ME
family	かぞく KA ZO KU
father	おとうさん O TO O SA N
February	二がつ / にがつ NI GA TSU
football	フットボール FU T TO BO O RU
French	フランスご FU RA N SU GO
Friday	金曜日 / きんようび KI N YO O BI
fried noodles	やきそば YA KI SO BA
friend	ともだち TO MO DA CHI
fun/enjoyable	たのしい TA NO SHI I
funny	おもしろい O MO SHI RO I
games	ゲーム GE E MU
goldfish	金ぎょ / きんぎょ KI N GYO
go	行きます / いきます I KI MA SU
good	いい I I
grade ...	…ねんせい NE N SE I
grandfather	おじいさん O JI I SA N
grandmother	おばあさん O BA A SA N
green	みどり MI DO RI
green tea	おちゃ O CHA
greeting used after introducing oneself	どおぞ よろしく DO O ZO YO RO SHI KU (おねがいします)。 O NE GA I SHI MA SU
hair	かみのけ KA MI NO KE
hamburger	ハンバーガー HA N BA A GA A
hello? (on phone)	もしもし MO SHI MO SHI
hello/good day	こんにちは KO N NI CHI WA
Here you are.	どうぞ。 DO O ZO
hobby	しゅみ SHU MI
Hokkaido	ほっかいどう HO K KA I DO O

WORDLIST – ENGLISH/JAPANESE	
ENGLISH	JAPANESE/ROOMAJI
home	うち U CHI
Honshu	本しゅう / ほんしゅう HO N SHU U
horse	うま U MA
hot	あつい A TSU I
hot dog	ホットドッグ HO T TO DO G GU
how many people?	何人 NA N NI N
how much	いくら I KU RA
I (used by boys)	ぼく BO KU
I (used mostly by girls)	わたし WA TA SHI
I'm pleased to meet you.	はじめまして。 HA JI ME MA SHI TE
ice-cream	アイスクリーム A I SU KU RI I MU
in (a season)	に NI
interesting/funny	おもしろい O MO SHI RO I
isn't it?	ね NE
January	一月 / いちがつ I CHI GA TSU
Japan	日本 / にほん / にっぽん NI HO N / NI P PO N
Japanese (language)	日本ご / にほんご NI HO N GO
Japanese (person)	日本人 / にほんじん NI HO N JI N
juice	ジュース JU U SU
Judo	じゅうどう JU U DO O
July	七月 / しちがつ SHI CHI GA TSU
June	六月 / ろくがつ RO KU GA TSU
kind	やさしい YA SA SI I
Kyushu	きゅうしゅう KYU U SHU U
later	あとで A TO DE
let me see ...	そうですね SO O DE SU NE
let's do/play	しましょう SHI MA SHO O
let's eat	たべましょう TA BE MA SHO O
let's go	行きましょう / いきましょう I KI MA SHO O
let's watch	見ましょう / みましょう MI MA SHO O
library	としょかん TO SHO KA N
like	すき SU KI
little	すこし SU KO SHI
March	三月 / さんがつ SA N GA TSU
May	五月 / ごがつ GO GA TSU
milk	ミルク MI RU KU
Monday	月曜日 / げつようび GE TSU YO O BI
monkey	さる SA RU
mouse/rat	ねずみ NE ZU MI
mother	おかあさん O KA A SA N
movie	えいが E I GA

WORDLIST – ENGLISH/JAPANESE	
ENGLISH	JAPANESE/ROOMAJI
music	おんがく O N GA KU
my (for boys)	ぼくの BO KU NO
my (for girls)	わたしの WA TA SHI NO
(my) name	なまえ NA MA E
(your) name	おなまえ O NA MA E
New Zealand	ニュージーランド NYU U JI I RA N DO
New Zealander (person)	ニュージーランド人 / ニュージーランドじん NYU U JI I RA N DO JI N
next week	らいしゅう RA I SHU U
no	いいえ I I E
no, I don't have	いいえ、いません I I E I MA SE N
No, it's boring.	いいえ、つまらないです。 I I E TSU MA RA NA I DE SU
noisy	うるさい U RU SA I
North America	きたアメリカ KI TA A ME RI KA
not at all	ぜんぜん ZE N ZE N
November	十一月 / じゅう いちがつ JU U I CHI GA TSU
number	ばんごう BA N GO O
October	十月 / じゅうがつ JU U GA TSU
often	よく YO KU
on (a day, e.g. Sunday)	に NI
Osaka	おおさか O O SA KA
person	人 / じん JI N
pants	ズボン ZU BO N
park	こうえん KO O E N
particle wa	は WA
person	人 / ひと / じん / にん HI TO / JI N / NI N
pet	ペット PE T TO
pizza	ピザ PI ZA
plane	ひこうき HI KO O KI
play/do	します SHI MA SU
played/did	しました SHI MA SHI TA
please	ください KU DA SA I
Please be quiet.	しずかにしてください。 SHI ZU KA NI SHI TE KU DA SA I.
Please close your book.	本をとじてください / ほん を とじて ください。 HO N O TO JI TE KU DA SA I.
Please listen.	きいてください。 KI I TE KU DA SA I.
Please look.	見てください / みて ください。 MI TE KU DA SA I.
Please open your book.	本をひらいてください / ほん を ひらいて ください。 HO N O HI RA I TE KU DA SA I.
Please phone.	でんわしてください。 DE N WA SHI TE KU DA SA I.
Please sit.	すわってください。 SU WA T TE KU DA SA I.
Please stand.	たってください。 TA T TE KU DA SA I.

WORDLIST – ENGLISH/JAPANESE	
ENGLISH	JAPANESE/ROOMAJI
question particle	か KA
rabbit	うさぎ U SA GI
read	よみます YO MI MA SU
read (past tense)	よみました YO MI MA SHI TA
reading (the hobby)	どくしょ DO KU SHO
red	あか A KA
restaurant	レストラン RE SU TO RA N
Russia	ロシア RO SHI A
Russian (person)	ロシアじん RO SHI A JI N
said after eating	ごちそうさまでした GO CHI SO O SA MA DE SHI TA
said before eating	いただきます I TA DA KI MA SU
sandwich	サンドイッチ SA N DO I T CHI
Saturday	土曜日 / どようび DO YO O BI
saw/watched	見ました / みました MI MA SHI TA
scary	こわい KO WA I
school	がっこう GA K KO O
sea/beach	うみ U MI
see/watch	見ます / みます MI MA SU
self introduction	じこしょうかい JI KO SHO O KA I
September	九月 / くがつ KU GA TSU
sheep	ひつじ HI TSU JI
Shikoku	しこく SHI KO KU
shirt	シャツ SHA TSU
shoes	くつ KU TSU
shop(s)	みせ MI SE
shopping	ショッピング SHO P PI N GU
sister (older)	おねえさん O NE E SA N
sister (younger)	いもうと I MO O TO
small	ちいさい CHI I SA I
snake	へび HE BI
soccer	サッカー SA K KA A
socks	くつした KU TSU SHI TA
sometimes	ときどき TO KI DO KI
South America	みなみアメリカ MI NA MI A ME RI KA
sport	スポーツ SU PO O TSU
sports field	グランド GU RA N DO
spring	春 / はる HA RU
studied/learnt	べんきょうしました BE N KYO O SHI MA SHI TA
study/learn	べんきょうします BE N KYO O SHI MA SU
summer	夏 / なつ NA TSU
Sunday	日曜日 / にちようび NI CHI YO O BI
swimming	すいえい SU I E I

WORDLIST – ENGLISH/JAPANESE	
ENGLISH	JAPANESE/ROOMAJI
TV	テレビ TE RE BI
tea (green)	おちゃ O CHA
teacher	せんせい SE N SE I
telephone (number)	でんわ DE N WA
tennis	テニス TE NI SU
Thank you very much.	ありがとうございます。 A RI GA TO O GO ZA I MA SU
that	それ SO RE
that over there	あれ A RE
this	これ KO RE
this year	今年 / ことし KO TO SHI
Thursday	木曜日 / もくようび MO KU YO O BI
tiger	とら TO RA
to (a place)	に NI
today	きょう KYO O
Tokyo	とうきょう TO O KYO O
tomorrow	あした A SHI TA
train	でんしゃ DE N SHA
Tuesday	火曜日 / かようび KA YO O BI
Umm ..., let me see	ええと… E E TO
uncle	おじさん O JI SA N
used after boy's name	くん KU N
used after girl's name	さん SA N
video game	テレビゲーム TE RE BI GE E MU
warm	あたたかい A TA TA KA I
was big	大きかったです / おおきかったです O O KI KA T TA DE SU
was boring	つまらなかったです TSU MA RA NA KA T TA DE SU
was cute	かわいかったです KA WA I KA T TA DE SU
was fun/enjoyable	たのしかったです TA NO SHI KA T TA DE SU
was good	よかったです YO KA T TA DE SU
was interesting/funny	おもしろかったです O MO SHI RO KA T TA DE SU
was small	小さかったです / ちいさかったです CHI I SA KA T TA DE SU
water	水 / みず MI ZU
water monster	かっぱ KA P PA
Wednesday	水曜日 / すいようび SU I YO O BI
weekend	しゅうまつ SHU U MA TSU
Welcome (to my shop).	いらっしゃいませ。 I RA S SHA I MA SE
well ...	じゃ JA
went	行きました / いきました I KI MA SHI TA
what	何 / なに / なん NA NI / NA N
what kind of	どんな DO N NA

WORDLIST – ENGLISH/JAPANESE	
ENGLISH	JAPANESE/ROOMAJI
what month	何月 / なんがつ NA N GA TSU
what nationality	何人 / なにじん NA NI JI N
what number	何ばん / なんばん NA N BA N
What birth year sign are you?	何年ですか / なにどしですか。 NA NI DO SHI DE SU KA
when	いつ I TSU
where	どこ DO KO
who	だれ DA RE
whose	だれの DA RE NO
white	しろ SHI RO
wild pig / boar	いのしし I NO SHI SHI
will phone	でんわします DE N WA SHI MA SU
winter	冬 / ふゆ FU YU
with (a person)	と TO
(your) birthday	おたんじょう日 / おたんじょうび O TA N JO O BI
(your) name	おなまえ O NA MA E
years old	さいです SA I DE SU
yellow	きいろ KI I RO
yen	えん E N
yes	はい HA I
yes, I do have	はい、います HA I I MA SU
yes, let's do that	はい、そうしましょう HA I SO O SHI MA SHO O
you (for boys)	name + くん KU N
you (for girls)	name + さん SA N
your (for boys)	name + くんの KU N NO
your (for girls)	name + さんの SA N NO
zero	ゼロ ZE RO
zoo	どうぶつえん DO O BU TSU E N

HIRAGANA CHARTS

あ A	い I	う U	え E	お O
か KA	き KI	く KU	け KE	こ KO
が GA	ぎ GI	ぐ GU	げ GE	ご GO
さ SA	し SHI	す SU	せ SE	そ SO
ざ ZA	じ JI	ず ZU	ぜ ZE	ぞ ZO
た TA	ち CHI	つ TSU	て TE	と TO
だ DA			で DE	ど DO
な NA	に NI	ぬ NU	ね NE	の NO
は HA	ひ HI	ふ FU	へ HE	ほ HO
ば BA	び BI	ぶ BU	べ BE	ぼ BO
ぱ PA	ぴ PI	ぷ PU	ぺ PE	ぽ PO
ま MA	み MI	む MU	め ME	も MO
や YA		ゆ YU		よ YO
ら RA	り RI	る RU	れ RE	ろ RO
わ WA				を O
ん N				

きゃ kya	きゅ kyu	きょ kyo
ぎゃ gya	ぎゅ gyu	ぎょ gyo
しゃ sha	しゅ shu	しょ sho
じゃ ja	じゅ ju	じょ jo
ちゃ cha	ちゅ chu	ちょ cho
にゃ nya	にゅ nyu	にょ nyo
ひゃ hya	ひゅ hyu	ひょ hyo
びゃ bya	びゅ byu	びょ byo
ぴゃ pya	ぴゅ pyu	ぴょ pyo
みゃ mya	みゅ myu	みょ myo
りゃ rya	りゅ ryu	りょ ryo

KATAKANA CHARTS

ア	イ	ウ	エ	オ
A	I	U	E	O
カ	キ	ク	ケ	コ
KA	KI	KU	KE	KO
ガ	ギ	グ	ゲ	ゴ
GA	GI	GU	GE	GO
サ	シ	ス	セ	ソ
SA	SHI	SU	SE	SO
ザ	ジ	ズ	ゼ	ゾ
ZA	JI	ZU	ZE	ZO
タ	チ	ツ	テ	ト
TA	CHI	TSU	TE	TO
ダ			デ	ド
DA			DE	DO
ナ	ニ	ヌ	ネ	ノ
NA	NI	NU	NE	NO
ハ	ヒ	フ	ヘ	ホ
HA	HI	FU	HE	HO
バ	ビ	ブ	ベ	ボ
BA	BI	BU	BE	BO
パ	ピ	プ	ペ	ポ
PA	PI	PU	PE	PO
マ	ミ	ム	メ	モ
MA	MI	MU	ME	MO
ヤ		ユ		ヨ
YA		YU		YO
ラ	リ	ル	レ	ロ
RA	RI	RU	RE	RO
ワ				ン
WA				N

キャ	キュ	キョ
kya	kyu	kyo
ギャ	ギュ	ギョ
gya	gyu	gyo
シャ	シュ	ショ
sha	shu	sho
ジャ	ジュ	ジョ
ja	ju	jo
チャ	チュ	チョ
cha	chu	cho
ニャ	ニュ	ニョ
nya	nyu	nyo
ヒャ	ヒュ	ヒョ
hya	hyu	hyo
ビャ	ビュ	ビョ
bya	byu	byo
ピャ	ピュ	ピョ
pya	pyu	pyo
ミャ	ミュ	ミョ
mya	myu	myo
リャ	リュ	リョ
rya	ryu	ryo

クァ	グァ	クィ	クェ	クォ
kwa	gwa	kwi	kwe	kwo
ティ	トゥ	ディ	ウェ	
ti	tu	di	ye	
ファ	フィ	フュ	フェ	フォ
fa	fi	fyu	fe	fo
シェ	ジェ	チェ		ヴォ
she	je	che		vo
ヴァ	ヴィ	ヴ	ヴュ	ヴェ
va	vi	vu	vyu	ve
ウィ	ウェ	ウォ		
wi	we	wo		

RULES FOR WRITING VERTICALLY USING GENKOOYOOSHI

When writing formal essays, it is usual to use squared paper (げんこうようし) and write downwards, starting from the top right-hand side. You don't have to leave spaces between words and you may continue to the top of the next row in the middle of a word. Look at the genkooyooshi grid below for other special features.

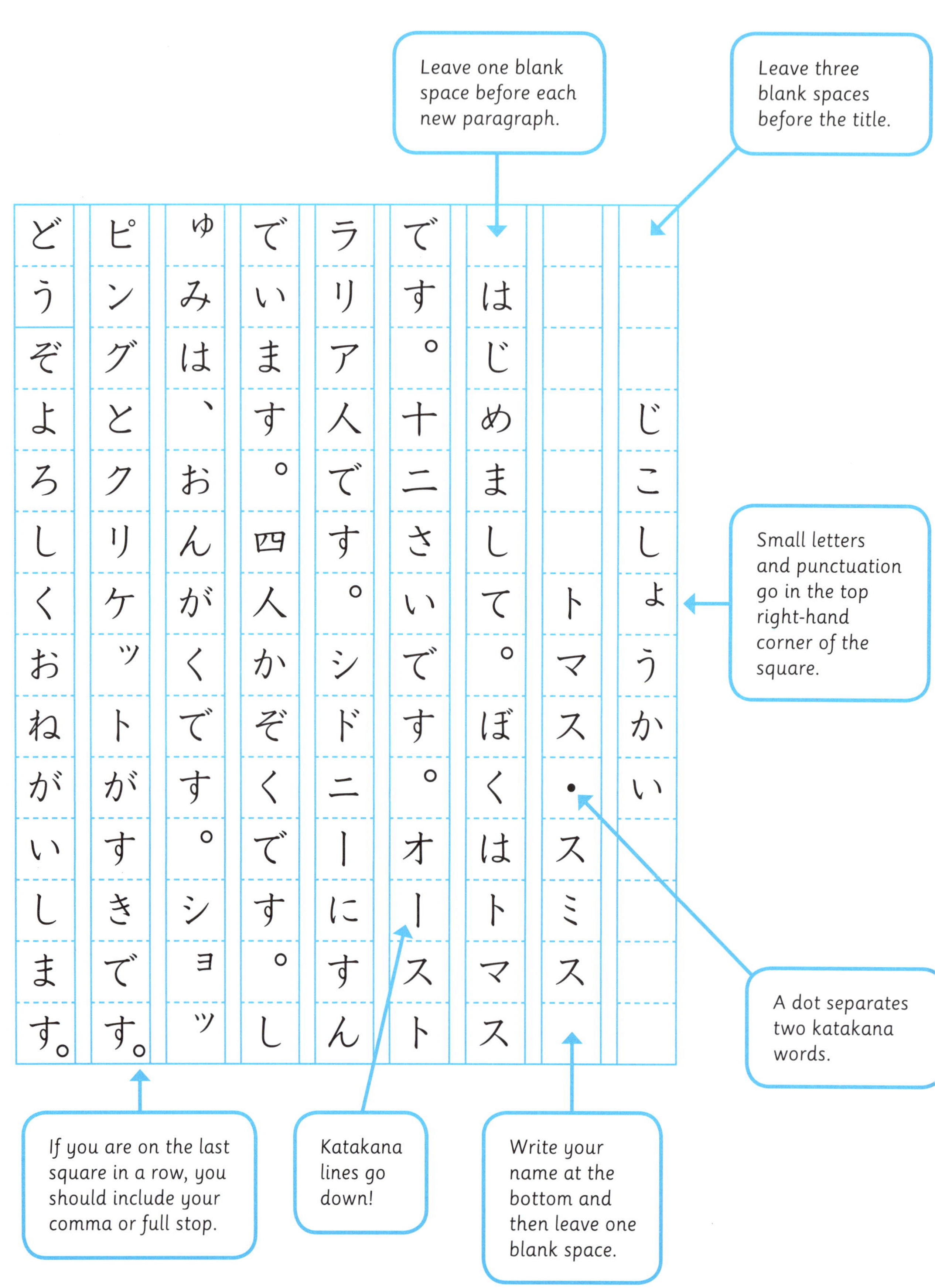